© 2019

Good Moms Have Bad Days:
Understanding Postpartum Mood Disorders

By Eren Simpson

For the fighters, the survivors, the grieving, the lost,
the hopeful ... **you are not alone.**

Table of Contents

i.

Introduction from the author

Hi. My name is Eren Simpson, and I'm a sufferer of postpartum depression/anxiety, which has since developed into major depressive disorder, possible BiPolar II, or just general impulse control disorder and generalized anxiety; aka, I'm a fucking mess.

I'm also a reporter by education and trade. Ever since I was little, I've wanted to be a writer and a reporter. In 2006, I graduated with a degree in Journalism from UNC-Chapel Hill. I worked as a reporter for six years before switching to non-profit work and freelancing, until I had kids. Then everything went to shit.

With both kids, I had horrible postpartum depression. The first time around, it wasn't diagnosed until my son was 1.

That entire first year of his life, I was exhausted, didn't have the energy to shower or fix my hair, and gave up eating anything I wanted or needed so I could continue to breastfeed my son, who was allergic to everything as a baby. I was a horrible mess. But any time someone mentioned it, I'd brush it off and say, "I'm just tired."

I didn't tell anyone that I beat my head repeatedly with my fist at night when I had to go back in to my son's room for the millionth feed of the day and was so angry at my son that I hit myself in order to redirect my anger. I didn't tell them I was terrified I was going to fall down the stairs every time I walked passed them on my way to his room. I didn't tell anyone that I leaned over his bassinette every night to see if he was still breathing, that I had nightmares I squished him in my sleep, or that I just was so afraid I was failing in every aspect of being a mom.

After I was diagnosed, one of my friends said, "Yeah, I wondered if you had postpartum depression then." But she never fucking said anything to me. She also had a newborn, so what was she supposed to do?

It was my husband that finally said, "I think you have postpartum depression. You're not just tired." I didn't want to hear it, but knowing how miserable I was, I Googled "postpartum help resources" on my phone while

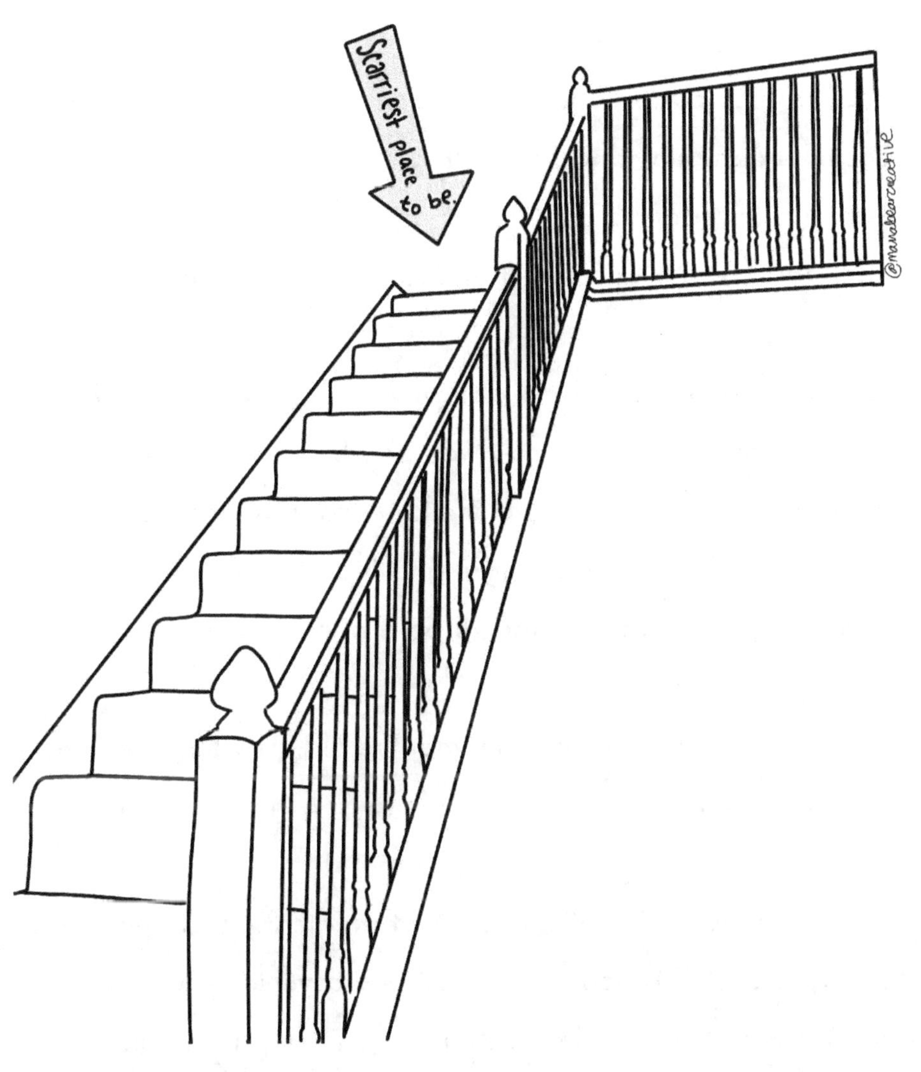

Stairiest place to be.
@nanabearcreative

breastfeeding my son one night. I made the call the next day and finally started to get some help.

Then I found out I was pregnant again.

I was on medication and in regular therapy all through my second pregnancy, and I felt OK. So when my daughter was born and I'd had the delivery of my dreams, I really thought I was going to be OK. But it ended up being so much worse.

During the first year of my daughter's life, I would beg my husband for a divorce, wish I was dead, threaten suicide, dream of driving away from the house and never coming home, and break down in tears and hide in my closet because I just couldn't stand to be around anyone.

When my daughter turned six months old, I switched her to formula and got on stronger meds to get through it all.

After trying what felt like dozens of medications, I ended up having to switch psychiatrists. My new psychiatrist diagnosed me with impulse disorder and anxiety. They put me on an anti-seizure medication plus an SSRI, eventually reducing me to just an SSRI and now I'm a mostly functional human being. But I'm still a work in progress in a major way.

I'm writing this book because in the first year of my daughter's life, we spent nearly $10,000 on getting me well.

That is what most people in the U.S. consider "inexpensive" when it comes to weddings and other superfluous shit, but it ate up half of our savings account and caused more marital fights than I could have ever imagined.

Why did it cost so much? Because all of the therapists I saw did not accept insurance – as they weren't being compensated fairly by the insurance companies – so everything was out of pocket. Because my OB/GYN failed to diagnose me during the postpartum check-ups. Because my children's pediatrician never asked. And because I had to switch my child to formula so I could go on medication that would actually help me.

These are costs that no family should have to incur or anticipate. Mental health care should not deplete a family's resources, and a woman should NEVER feel, "It would have been cheaper if I killed myself," something I've repeated more times than I can count in the last two years.

To write this book has been triggering, to say the least. But I felt like it was absolutely necessary, because while postpartum mood disorders are becoming less taboo to talk about, there's still a lot of misinformation, and there's still so much not being done to take care of women postpartum.

So, I'm writing this book from the position of reporter and patient. I've been there, I'm there right now, and I've been doing my homework. I hope this book gives sufferers, caregivers, and anyone else affected by these disorders a one-stop shop (or at least a starting point) for information and serves as a launching pad for us to do something about it.

If you've picked up this book, I'm sorry. BUT, you've come to the right place, you CAN figure this out, you WILL beat this, and you ARE 100 percent WORTH THIS FIGHT!

ii.

Emergency resources

If you're feeling suicidal, text the crisis hotline and someone will speak with you immediately. Text CONNECT to 741741.

The following resources have been compiled from Postpartum Support International – an organization dedicated to supporting postpartum women and families. (6/12/19*)

*Call or text the PSI HelpLine

Available 24 hours a day. You will be asked to leave a confidential message, and a trained and caring volunteer will return your call or text. They will listen, answer questions, offer encouragement, and connect you with local resources as needed.

Call 1-800-944-4773 (4PPD) or text 503-894-9453 (English and Spanish)

***Use the PSI support locator**

Find counselors and therapists in your area that can help:

https://www.postpartum.net/get-help/locations/ or call 1-800-944-4773.

***Join an online support group**

https://www.supportgroupscentral.com/groups_detail.cfm?cid=17&CFID=722078&CFTOKEN=4b71119966239c09-F98A3021-D438-4599-29A1840420EE1C0B

***Chat with an expert**

Wednesday chats for moms and First Monday chats for dad.

During these sessions you can connect with other moms and dads, and you can talk with a PSI expert about resources, symptoms, options, and general information about perinatal mood and anxiety disorders from the privacy of your own phone. There is no need to pre-register or give your name.

These sessions, facilitated by licensed mental health professionals, are informational only and open to anyone with questions and concerns. They are limited to the first 15 callers.

Please note: The bridge line will stop accepting callers

when the maximum of 15 callers has been reached. Sessions will last approximately one hour. These chats are not meant to take the place of needed visits to healthcare providers and do not provide therapy.

Chat number: 1-800-944-8766, participant code 73162

Please see the website for their up-to-date schedules:

https://www.postpartum.net/get-help/chat-with-an-expert/

*Join the Smart Patients Forum

Postpartum Support International has partnered with @smartpatientscommunity, an online forum for women affected by #PPD.

You can join the community for free to share, interact, and learn from peers in a safe and supportive environment. To learn more or join today, visit www.smartpatients.com/psi.

Inpatient perinatal psychiatry programs in the U.S.

North Carolina

UNC Perinatal Psychiatry Inpatient Unit

UNC School of Medicine, Department of Psychiatry

Phone: 984-974-5217, option 3

New York

Northwell Health Perinatal Psychiatry Services

Northwell Health, Obstetrics and Gynecology

Phone: 888-321-3627 (DOCS)

Outpatient and partial hospitalization perinatal psychiatric support programs in the U.S.

California

- El Camino Hospital Maternal Outreach Mood Services (MOMS)

  Mountain View. Phone: 1-800-216-5556

- Hoag Hospital Maternal Mental Health Clinic

  Newport Beach. Phone: 949-764-5333

- Huntington Memorial Hospital Maternal Wellness Program

  Pasadena. Phone: 626-397-5000

- UC San Diego Women's Reproductive Mental Health Program

  La Jolla, Hillcrest, and Sorrento Valley. Phone: 858-534-7792 (PSYC)

- <u>UCLA Maternal Mental Health Program at Resnick Neuropsychiatric Hospital</u>
  Los Angeles. Phone: 310-825-4138

Florida

- <u>Better Beginnings Mother/Baby Partial Hospitalization Program</u>
  Alachua. Phone: 352-462-9484

Illinois

- <u>AMITA Health Perinatal Intensive Outpatient Program at Alexian Brothers Women & Children's Hospital</u>
  Hoffman Estates. Phone: 847-755-3220

Michigan

- <u>Pine Rest Mother and Baby Program</u>
  Grand Rapids. Phone: 1-800-678-5500

Minnesota

- <u>Hennepin Mother-Baby Day Hospital</u>
  Minneapolis. Phone: 612-873-6262 (MAMA)

- <u>PrairieCare Perinatal Mental Health Clinic</u>
  Brooklyn Park. Phone: 612-274-7494

- <u>Nystrom Counseling Mother Baby Intensive Outpatient Program</u>
  Baxter/Brainerd, Eden Prairie, and Ostego. Phone: 651-419-4332

Missouri

- <u>Mercy Birthplace Mother-Baby Intensive Outpatient Program</u>
  St. Louis. Phone: 314-251-6500

New Jersey

- <u>Monmouth Medical Center Perinatal Mood & Anxiety Disorders Program</u>
  Long Branch. Phone: 732-923-5573

New York

- <u>The Motherhood Center of New York Day Program</u>
  Manhattan. Phone: 212-335-0034

Pennsylvania

- <u>Drexel University Mother Baby Connections Intensive Outpatient Program</u>
  Philadelphia. Phone: 267-282-1455

- <u>Alexis Joy D'Achille Center for Perinatal Mental Health at West Penn Hospital</u>
  Pittsburgh. Phone: 412-362-8677

Rhode Island

- <u>Brown/Women & Infants Day Hospital Program</u>
  Providence. Phone: 401-453-7955

Utah

- <u>Serenity Recovery and Wellness</u>
  Riverton and Provo. Phone: 801-984-0184

- <u>Reach Counseling</u>
  South Jordan. Phone: 801-446-3515

- <u>St. Mark's Hospital Perinatal Outpatient Program</u>
  Salt Lake City. Phone: 801-268-7438

Washington

- <u>Swedish Center for Perinatal Bonding and Support</u>
  Seattle. Phone: 206-320-7288

Support for Spanish-speaking families
Apoyo de PSI para las familias Hispano parlantes

Llame al número de teléfono gratuito para obtener recursos, apoyo e información gratuita. Déjenos un mensaje y un voluntario le devolverá la llamada. Podrá encontrar más información y recursos en la página web de PSI, presione en el botón siguiente.

Teléfono: 1-800-944-4773, #1

https://www.postpartum.net/en-espanol/

Call the toll-free Phone line, select #1, for resources, support, and information. Leave us a message, and one of our support volunteers will call you back. We also have Online Resources on the PSI website.

Telephone: 1-800-944-4773, #1

https://www.postpartum.net/en-espanol/

Support for Arabic-speaking families

- Nadia Abdulla

  Nadia provides email and telephone support, and she can help you find resources in your country.

  Telephone: 004369911941710

Support for military families

Weekly online support group:

https://www.postpartum.net/get-help/psi-online-support-meetings/

Army

- Melinda Thiam

  Phone: 803-851-0642 or 803-446-5252

  melinda.thiam.psi@gmail.com

- Allie Kelley

  Phone: 601-946-6100 (call or text)

  alliemoses@hotmail.com

Coast Guard

- Shawna Bush

  Phone: 847-970-8750 (call or text)

  Wagnersm89@gmail.com

Navy and Marine Corp

- Melissa Nauss

  Phone: (504) 534-5496 (call or text)

  PSIMilitaryCoordinator@gmail.com

- Raquel Harp

  Please note Raquel is in Hawaii.

  Phone: 281-541-4772 (call or text)

  Raquelvharp@gmail.com

Air Force

- Marit Watson

  Phone: 707-474-8805 (call or text)

  MWatson.PSI@gmail.com

- Carrie Chalverus

  Phone: 702-588-3804

  cchalverus@gmail.com

- Kate Mixon

  Phone: 540-429-5905

  kemixon@gmail.com

National Guard

- Brandie Judy

  Phone: (681) 214-0305 (call or text)

  BrandiePSI2018@gmail.com

If you would like to volunteer to provide support or resources to military families, please contact Carrie Banks at cbanks@postpartum.net

****IMPORTANT: Some of these resources may have changed by the time this book is published. For the most up-to-date listing, please visit www.postpartum.net for their comprehensive lists.**

iii.

How to read this book

Dear reader, I hope you are finding and reading this book before you need it. If I'd found this book at the height of my struggle, I don't know that I would have heard everything it had to say.

So, if you are newly diagnosed, I would start by reading the stories of the other women in chapter eight who have struggled with a postpartum mood disorder so that you know you're not alone.

If you are undiagnosed but feel like you may have a postpartum mood disorder, please read chapters four, five, six, and seven to figure out where you fit in the spectrum and where you should go for help. You can also see the resource guide in section ii for immediate help.

If you are pregnant, read from the beginning, because I just want every man and woman out there to be prepared.

Facing and being diagnosed with a postpartum mood disorder is often terrifying, sometimes debilitating, and is a discouraging, frustrating, and maddening experience. I want you to know that there is help out there. There are women and families who have been through it, and that the thoughts and feelings you are having are COMPLETELY NORMAL. They're scary, yes, but you're not a bad mom (or dad, because men can experience these feelings too) for having them. They will go away and then creep back in, and then hopefully they'll eventually disappear completely and this nightmare will be just a distant memory. It's best to be prepared and armed with the knowledge of where to go for help, who to talk to about your problems, and what signs to look for. Also make sure you're on the same page with your loved ones on how to deal with these things if and when they come up.

Chapter 1:

What hormones are doing to your body during and after pregnancy

Everyone knows your hormones go nuts during pregnancy. Here are the main hormones at play during those nine months:

The **human chorionic gonadotropin** hormone (HCG) is made almost exclusively in the placenta and is what causes that double pink line or plus sign on your pregnancy test. Your HCG levels rise a lot during the first trimester. They may play a part in the nausea and vomiting often linked to pregnancy.

The **human placental lactogen** hormone (HPL) is also known as the human chorinic somatomammotropin and is made by the placenta. It gives nutrition to the fetus and stimulates milk glands in the breasts for breastfeeding.

Estrogen is the group of hormones that helps develop the female sexual traits and is normally formed in the ovaries.

It is also made by the placenta to help maintain a healthy pregnancy.

Progesterone is made by the ovaries and by the placenta during pregnancy. It stimulates the thickening of the uterine lining for implantation of a fertilized egg.

Info is from Johns Hopkins

Once you give birth, all of these hormones (plus that delicious oxytocin released when doing skin-to-skin contact, breastfeeding, etc.) make you feel like everything is amazing and wonderful, and you're soooooo in love with this little creature you just expelled from your body – whether vaginally or surgically. You are a magical goddess, and you can do anything.

These are your endorphins (and that oxytocin) speaking. These are those feel-good hormones that you can get from a really good run or Zumba class, and they are running on high for the first 24-hours after you gift birth.

But by day three or four, your hormones take a serious nosedive. After your body releases the placenta, all the hormones it was producing – such as estrogen, progesterone,

relaxin, HCG, and HPL - go with it.

At this point, your estrogen and progesterone are the lowest they will ever be until you hit menopause. Fun, huh?! This is when many women start feeling those post-baby blues; they're sad, weepy, and just in a funk. Day three is when that sleep deprivation hits, once the adrenaline has worn off. Sleep deprivation is very clearly linked to cortisol, the stress hormone. This also impacts the way you feel, and it can seem like you're being tortured in Guantanamo. But hopefully you've got oxytocin coursing through your system from quality baby time, which can help with some of the postpartum sadness (unless you're one of the unlucky ones, which is why you're reading this book).

For approximately eight percent of women in Canada (and 15 percent in the U.S.), those baby blues will turn into postpartum depression or another postpartum mood disorder. Because as you may or not know, depression isn't the only postpartum disorder affecting women.

While breastfeeding may help some women increase their oxytocin and other hormones that help boost their mood, for others - like me - it can increase their risk for postpartum depression. One large study of over 2,500 women found that women who had negative breastfeeding experiences were more likely to have symptoms of depression:

> *Compared with Women with no early neonatal signs of breastfeeding difficulty, we found that women who had negative feelings about breastfeeding and reported severe pain while nursing soon after birth were more likely to experience postpartum depression at two months.*

In the United States, statistics show that only 25 percent of mothers exclusively breastfeed their infants for the recommended minimum six months, and ten percent of new mothers experience postpartum depression.

Another study published in Maternal and Child Health Journal found that the effect of breastfeeding on postpartum mental health differed according to whether the woman had planned during her pregnancy to breastfeed her infant or not. Women who had intended to breastfeed their infant but who were unable to breastfeed postpartum had higher rates of postpartum depression.

Maybe you're like me and planned on breastfeeding, fought tooth and nail to be able to continue - much to your own detriment – and you still ended up with horrific postpartum depression and anxiety. Not everyone's body reacts the same way to hormones. What's good for one might be horrible for another, so please try not to compare yourself to other moms. The "lucky moms" as you may look at it are wrestling with their own demons. We've all got them.

So what role do hormones play in the diagnosis of a postpartum mood disorder? No one really knows, and there are clinical trials going on right now to figure it out. An article from Johns Hopkins Medicine says symptoms of postpartum depression could be related to a hormone our body produces (or doesn't) in the second trimester.

In the article, titled "Hormone Levels May Predict Postpartum Depression," the authors mention a small-scale study conducted of women who'd been previously diagnosed with a mood disorder. The study found that having lower levels of the hormone **allopregnanolone** is associated with an increased chance of developing postpartum mood disorders in women already known to be at risk. This may not mean much for anyone who hasn't previously had a history of mental health disorders.

But in another report on the study, published online

FORMULA
FED IS BEST

in *Psychoneuroendocrinology* on March 7, 2018, researchers say the findings could lead to diagnostic markers and preventive strategies for the condition, which strikes an estimated 15 to 20 percent of American women who give birth.

The researchers caution that theirs was an observational study in women already diagnosed with mood disorder and/or taking antidepressants or mood stabilizers, and does not establish cause and effect between the progesterone metabolite and postpartum depression. But it does, they say, add to evidence the hormonal disruptions during pregnancy point to opportunities for intervention.

Postpartum depression affects early bonding between the mother and child. Untreated, it has potentially devastating and even lethal consequences for both. Infants of women with the disorder may be neglected and may have trouble eating, sleeping, and developing normally (but not always, so don't let this linger in your mind). <u>An estimated 20 percent of postpartum maternal deaths are thought to be due to suicide, according to the National Institute of Mental Health.</u>

For the study, 60 pregnant women between the ages of 18 and 45 were recruited by investigators at study sites at Johns Hopkins University and the University of North Carolina at Chapel Hill. About 70 percent were white, and 21.5 percent were African-American. All women had been previously

"Many earlier studies haven't shown postpartum depression to be tied to actual levels of pregnancy hormones, but rather to an individual's vulnerability to fluctuations in these hormones, and they didn't identify any concrete way to tell whether a woman would develop postpartum depression," says Lauren M. Osborne, M.D., assistant director of the Johns Hopkins Women's Mood Disorders Center and assistant professor of psychiatry and behavioral sciences at the Johns Hopkins University School of Medicine. "For our study, we looked at a high-risk population of women already diagnosed with mood disorders and asked what might be making them more susceptible."

diagnosed with a mood disorder, such as major depression or bipolar disorder. Almost a third had been previously hospitalized due to complications from their mood disorder, and 73 percent had more than one mental illness.

During the study, 76 percent of the participants used psychiatric medications, including antidepressants or mood stabilizers. About 75 percent of the participants were depressed at some point during the investigation, either during the pregnancy or shortly thereafter.

During the second trimester (about 20 weeks pregnant) and the third trimester (about 34 weeks pregnant), each participant took a mood test and gave 40 milliliters of blood. 40 participants participated in the second-trimester data collection, and 19 of these women (47.5 percent) developed postpartum depression at one or three months postpartum. The participants were assessed and diagnosed by a clinician using criteria from the Diagnostic and Statistical Manual of Mental Disorders, Version IV, for a major depressive episode.

Of the 58 women who participated in the third-trimester data collection, 25 (43.1 percent) developed postpartum depression. 38 women participated in both trimester data collections

Using the blood samples, researchers measured the levels of progesterone and allopregnanolone, a byproduct made from the breakdown of progesterone that is known for its calming, anti-anxiety effects.

The researchers found no relationship between progesterone levels in the second or third trimesters and the likelihood of developing postpartum depression. They also found no link between the third-trimester levels of allopregnanolone and postpartum depression. <u>However, they did notice a link between postpartum depression and diminished levels of allopregnanolone levels in the second trimester.</u>

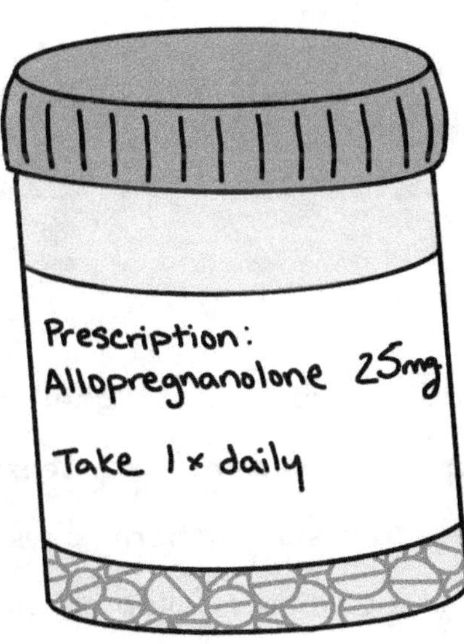

For example, according to the study data, a woman with an allopregnanolone level of 7.5 nanograms per milliliter had a 1.5 percent chance of developing postpartum depression. At half that level of hormone (about 3.75 nanograms per milliliter), a mother had a 33 percent likelihood of developing the disorder. For every additional nanogram per milliliter increase in allopregnanolone, the risk of developing postpartum depression dropped by 63 percent.

"Every woman has high levels of certain hormones, including allopregnanolone, at the end of pregnancy, so we decided to look earlier in the pregnancy to see if we could tease apart small differences in hormone levels that might more accurately predict postpartum depression later," says Osborne. She says that many earlier studies on postpartum depression focused on a less ill population, often excluding women whose symptoms were serious enough to warrant psychiatric medication — making it difficult to detect trends in those women most at risk.

Because the study data suggest that higher levels of allopregnanolone in the second trimester seem to protect against postpartum depression, Osborne says in the future, her group hopes to study whether allopregnanolone can be used in women at risk to prevent postpartum depression.

She says Johns Hopkins University is one of several institutions currently participating in a clinical trial led by Sage Therapeutics that is looking at allopregnanolone as a treatment for postpartum depression.

She also cautions that additional and larger studies are needed to determine whether women without mood disorders show the same patterns of allopregnanolone levels linked to postpartum depression risk.

If those future studies confirm a similar impact, Osborne says, then tests for low levels of allopregnanolone in the second trimester could be used as a biomarker to predict those mothers who are at risk of developing postpartum depression. In *Neuropsychopharmacology* in 2016, Osborne and her colleagues showed and replicated that epigenetic modifications to two genes could be used as biomarkers to predict postpartum depression. These modifications target genes that work with estrogen receptors and are sensitive to hormones.

These biomarkers were already about 80 percent effective at predicting postpartum depression, and Osborne hopes to examine whether combining allopregnanolone levels with the epigenetic biomarkers may improve the effectiveness of tests to predict postpartum depression.

Of note and seemingly contradictory, she says, many of the participants in the study developed postpartum depression while on antidepressants or mood stabilizers. The researchers say that the medication dosages weren't prescribed by the study group and were monitored by the participant's primary care physician, psychiatrist or obstetrician instead.

"We believe that many, if not most, women who become pregnant are undertreated for their depression because many physicians believe that smaller doses of antidepressants are safer for the baby, but we don't have any evidence that this is true," says Osborne. *"If the medication dose is too low and the mother relapses into depression during pregnancy or the postpartum period, then the baby will be exposed to both the drugs and the mother's illness."*

Osborne and her team are currently analyzing the medication dosages used by women in this study to determine whether those given adequate doses of antidepressants were less likely to develop symptoms in pregnancy or in postpartum. They are also looking in a new group of women that includes both healthy controls and those with major depression to see if they get the same results.

Only **15 percent** of women with postpartum depression are estimated to ever receive professional treatment, according to the U.S. Centers for Disease Control and Prevention. Many physicians don't screen for it, and there is a stigma for mothers. A mother who asks for help may be seen as incapable of handling her situation as a mother, or she may be criticized by friends or family for taking a medication during or shortly after pregnancy.

Additional authors on the study include Fiona Gispen, Abanti Sanyal, Gayane Yenokyan, Samantha Meilman, and Jennifer L. Payne of The Johns Hopkins University.

The study was funded by a grant from the National Institute of Mental Health (K23 MH074799).

*That was a lot, I know, and it was mostly OK to skim. I wanted you to know there are doctors out there working on making this easier to diagnose, predict, and treat. We gotta have hope and we gotta keep supporting the doctors and institutions doing this kind of research.

Chapter 2:

How did this happen to me, you, us?

We just got lucky, I guess. Isn't that what it feels like to you? "Why the fuck did this happen to me?!" The short answer is … I don't know. But, according to the National Institute of Mental Health (NIMH), it's more complicated than that.

First of all, one in nine women **(ONE IN NINE!!!)** in the United States is diagnosed with some type of postpartum mood disorder. That is a staggering number, considering how many women feel so alone in this diagnosis. So just sit with that for a second and remind yourself that you are not alone.

Second, postpartum depression and other postpartum mood disorders do not have a single cause, but they likely result from a combination of physical (see hormones in chapter one) and emotional factors. <u>Postpartum depression does not occur because of something a mother does or does not do.</u>

After childbirth, the levels of hormones (estrogen and

progesterone) in a woman's body quickly drop. This leads to chemical changes in her brain that may trigger mood swings. In addition, many mothers are unable to get the rest they need to fully recover from giving birth. Constant sleep deprivation can lead to physical discomfort and exhaustion, which can contribute to the symptoms of postpartum depression as we discussed in chapter one.

The NIMH says that some women are at greater risk for developing postpartum depression because they have one or more risk factors, such as:

- Symptoms of depression during or after a previous pregnancy

- Previous experience with depression or bipolar disorder

- A family member who has been diagnosed with depression or other mental illness.

- A stressful life event during pregnancy or shortly after giving birth, such as a job loss, death of a loved one, domestic violence, or personal illness

- Medical complications during childbirth, including premature (or traumatic) delivery or having a baby with medical problems

- Mixed feelings about the pregnancy, whether it was planned or unplanned

- A lack of strong emotional support from her spouse, partner, family, or friends

- Alcohol or other drug abuse problems

But the NIMH stresses that postpartum depression and mood disorders can affect any woman, regardless of mental health history, age, race, ethnicity, or economic status.

Who knows why you're dealing with this? Every person's experience with these mood disorders is different. I know it's hard to find comfort in the fact that you're not alone, especially if you don't have friends or family in close proximity who have dealt with these issues. But keep reading, or skip ahead to the section on building your support network and learn how to build a buffer around yourself that is going to make it easier to deal with this living nightmare.

Chapter 3:

Screening guidelines and recommendations

*Author's note: If you're reading this, you've likely already been let down by the postpartum/prenatal screening process for depression, anxiety, and other mood disorders, which is super frustrating. However, I felt it was important that I make available to you the screening guidelines that are currently out there, so that you can be aware of them for your next pregnancy, or so you can help out your friends and make sure they know what to ask for at their appointments. We've got to start doing better to support other mothers.

There is no more vulnerable time for mothers, fathers, and children than during pregnancy and postpartum, when psychiatric admissions rise higher than at any other time in a woman's life. **Postpartum depression is the most under-diagnosed obstetric complication in the U.S.** (Earls, 2010). Because the burden of depression and other mental health distress is so high for mothers and their children - and because it is often overlooked - Postpartum Support

International believes that there is a tremendous need for universal screening of all pregnant and postpartum women. Emotional stress and perinatal mental health disorders such as prenatal and postpartum depression and anxiety are clinically defined, treatable, and amenable to support, education, and intervention. Although there is increasing awareness of the rates of perinatal mental health disorders and the potential negative impact on mothers, babies, and families, perinatal mental health is far too often undiagnosed, under-treated, or not treated at all.

Postpartum Support International (PSI) recommends universal screening for the presence of prenatal or postpartum mood and anxiety disorders, using an evidence-based tool such as the Edinburgh Postnatal Depression Screen (EPDS) or Patient Health Questionnaire (PHQ-9).

Both the EPDS and the PHQ-9 are validated for use in the perinatal population, and there is no fee. (You can fill out and copy the tests – in Spanish and in English – in the back of this book). The questionnaires are self-administered, translated into many languages, and easy to complete. The EPDS addresses the anxiety component of PMADs, as well as depressive symptoms and suicidal thoughts. The PHQ-9 does not have the anxiety component but includes suicidal ideation. The PHQ-9 also incorporates the categories that define depression in the Diagnostic and Statistical Manual (DSM). With anxiety being recognized as one of the presenting symptoms of PMADs, it becomes important that it be assessed in the screening tool, making the EPDS the most widely used tool (Screening for Perinatal Depression. ACOG. 2015).

Understanding that healthcare settings are often very busy and providers feel pressured to complete appointments, Postpartum Support International recommends that providers learn efficient ways to screen patients and work toward these ideal practices:

Timing

- First prenatal visit

- At least once in second trimester

- At least once in third trimester

- Six-week postpartum obstetrical visit (or at first postpartum visit)

- Repeated screening at six and/or 12 months in OB and primary care settings

- Three, nine, and 12 month pediatric visits

If your doctor does not do these checks during those visits, MAKE THEM. You're paying them.

Tools

- EPDS (Edinburgh Postnatal Depression Scale) and PHQ-9 (Patient Health Questionnaire-9)

- The recommended cut-off score for a positive screen using either tool is ten.

- The EPDS is a reliable and valid measure of mood in fathers. Screening for depression or anxiety disorders in fathers requires a cut-off score that is two points lower than the cut-off score during screening for depression or anxiety in mothers. We recommend this cut-off to be five or six. (Matthey. 2001)

Setting

- PSI recommends universal screening in prenatal, postnatal, and pediatric settings.

- Settings for maternal mental health screening may

include, but are not limited to:

- *Healthcare providers (primary care, OB, midwifery, and pediatric)*

- *Public health*

- *Addictions and mental health*

- *Community social services*

- *Early childhood programs*

Administration

- Ideally, the self-report screening questionnaire should be provided in a private setting.

- It should be introduced and interpreted by a practitioner in a caring and informative manner that normalizes perinatal mental health needs.

- If possible, screening should be provided in the client's native language.

System

- Screening must exist in a system of care that includes educated providers, social support for families, and a protocol to follow up with those who have screened above the cut-off score on an evidence-based screening tool, aligned with the ACOG and USPSTF recommendations.

It is the goal of PSI to develop and nurture an integrated system of care that creates a safety net for parents and providers. All women should be screened routinely by their healthcare providers during and in the months following pregnancy. Women should ideally have access to reproductive psychiatric specialists in their community who can treat them, follow them, and coordinate care with OB providers, midwives, and pediatricians.

Resources

Postpartum Support International exists to help families and providers become informed and find resources they need to adequately screen, assess, refer, and follow up. Contact PSI at www.postpartum.net, or call 800-944-4PPD for up-to-date information, support, training, and resources.

Background on screening guidelines

Mandatory depression screening of pregnant and postpartum women is now recommended by an increasing number of professional organizations, including the

American College of Obstetrics and Gynecology (ACOG, 2015), the American Academy of Pediatrics (2010), and the American Medical Association, following the 2016 recommendation from the United States Preventive Services Task Force.

In May 2015, the ACOG recommended that screening for perinatal mood changes take place at least once during the perinatal period, including pregnancy and 12 months postpartum. This was a shift for the ACOG, and it speaks to the evolving research regarding perinatal mood disorders. The ACOG acknowledges that screening by itself does not improve outcomes. It is necessary to have a system in place that couples screening with appropriate follow-up and treatment. The recommendation included training front-line OB providers to recognize PMADs and be prepared to initiate treatment and referral to behavioral health providers.

Additionally, in January 2016, the U.S. Preventive Services Task Force (USPSTF) updated its 2009 recommendation related to screening for depression to include pregnant and postpartum women, adding to the consensus on screening in the perinatal period and supporting the recommendation of PSI.

*Again, it is important to note that these are the healthcare industry recommendations, and more and more professionals are observing them. However, there are still a lot of OB/GYNs who don't see it as their responsibility to handle this issue. Maybe it's a liability thing, or a billability thing with insurance - I don't know. But I know I and other women have been let down. The only time I was screened for postpartum mood disorders was less than 24 hours after my son and daughter were born in the hospital. I didn't feel sad at that point, of course. My body had just pushed out a human being, and we were both alive and well. What was there to be sad about? For the first year of my son's life, my mood kept getting worse, but the doctors never asked at my checkups. When I reported feeling increasingly stressed and agitated during a checkup, my doctor said, "Well, you're tired and stressed, but you want to treat the cause and not the symptoms." When I asked for help and an increase in medication, they just said, "You should call a psychiatrist," which was overwhelming and disheartening. I broke down in tears.

I didn't know where to start. That struggle is why I wrote this book. I believe no woman should be turned away by her OB/GYN when she expresses concern over her mental health, and I believe the resources to get help shouldn't be hard to find or access. There's only so much I can do as an author, but my hope is that I am giving you the tools to help yourself and your loved ones. These diseases are not to be made light of or ignored.

Chapter 4:

The different types of postpartum mood disorders, how they're similar, how they're different, how they're diagnosed, and treatment options for each.

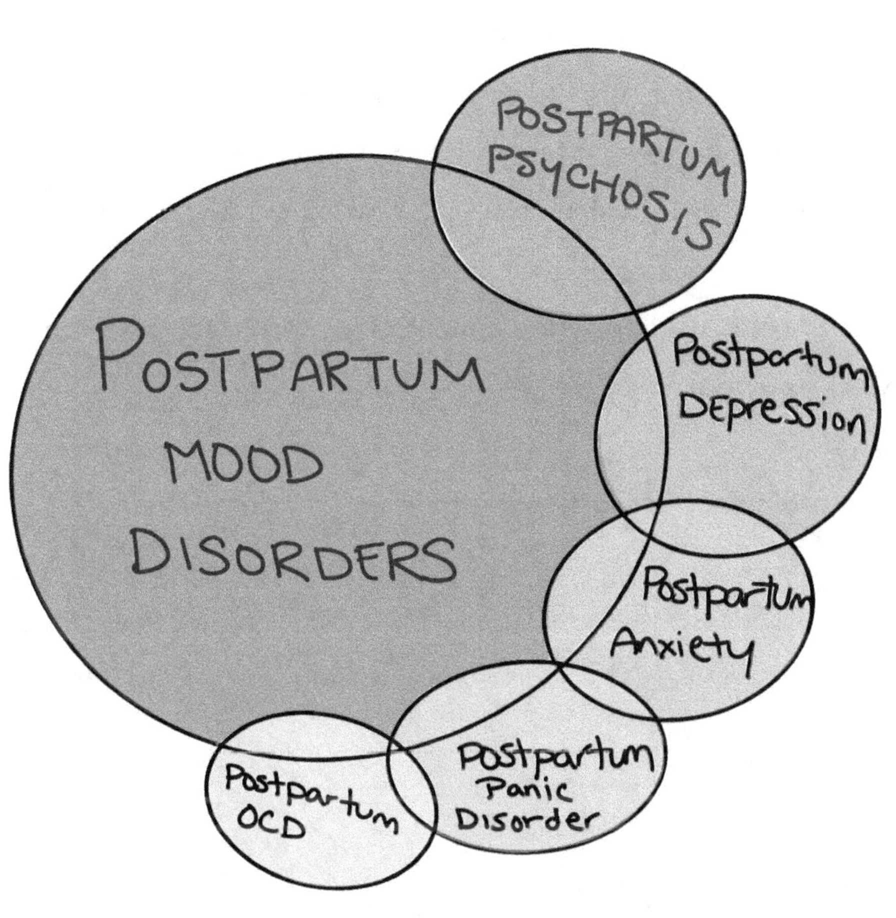

POSTPARTUM PSYCHOSIS
Postpartum Depression
Postpartum Anxiety
POSTPARTUM MOOD DISORDERS
Postpartum OCD
Postpartum Panic Disorder

Postpartum psychosis

The most worrisome of the postpartum mood disorders is postpartum psychosis. According to Postpartum Support International, postpartum psychosis is a rare illness compared to the rates of postpartum depression or anxiety. It occurs in approximately one or two out of every 1,000 deliveries, or approximately .1 percent -.2 percent of births.

The onset is usually sudden, most often within the first two weeks postpartum.

Symptoms of postpartum psychosis can include:

- Delusions or strange beliefs

- Hallucinations (seeing or hearing things that aren't there)

- Feeling very irritated

- Hyperactivity

- Decreased need for or inability to sleep

- Paranoia and suspiciousness

- Rapid mood swings

- Difficulty communicating at times

The most significant risk factors for postpartum psychosis are a personal or family history of bipolar disorder or a previous psychotic episode.

Research suggests there is approximately a five percent suicide rate and a four percent infanticide rate associated with postpartum psychosis. This is because the woman experiencing psychosis is experiencing a break from reality. In her psychotic state, delusions and unrealistic beliefs make sense to her; they feel very real to her and are often religious. <u>Immediate treatment for a woman going through psychosis is imperative.</u>

It is also important to know that many survivors of postpartum psychosis never had delusions containing violent commands. Delusions take many forms, and not all of them are destructive. <u>Most women who experience postpartum psychosis do not harm themselves or anyone else.</u> However, there is always the risk of danger. Psychosis includes delusional thinking and irrational judgment. This is why women with psychosis must be quickly assessed, treated, and carefully monitored by a trained perinatal mental health professional.

Postpartum psychosis is temporary and treatable with

professional help, but it is an emergency, and it is essential that you receive immediate help. If you feel you or someone you know may be suffering from this illness, know that it is not your fault and you are not to blame. Call your doctor or an emergency crisis hotline right away so you can get the help you need.

PSI has a **Postpartum Psychosis Coordinator** to provide additional assistance to women and families who are not in an emergency situation. Contact **Michele Davidson at 703-298-3247**, or at michelerdavidson@gmail.com.

In an emergency, call the emergency hotline: *1-800-273-8255*.

Postpartum depression

The most commonly talked about postpartum mood disorder is postpartum depression.

According to the Mayo Clinic, postpartum depression may be mistaken for baby blues at first. The signs and symptoms are more intense and last longer, however, and may eventually interfere with your ability to care for your baby and handle other daily tasks.

Symptoms usually develop within the first few weeks after giving birth but may begin earlier (during pregnancy) or later (up to a year after birth).

Postpartum depression signs and symptoms may include:

- Depressed mood or severe mood swings

- Excessive crying

- Difficulty bonding with your baby

- Withdrawing from family and friends

- Loss of appetite or eating much more than usual

- Inability to sleep (insomnia) or sleeping too much

- Overwhelming fatigue or loss of energy

- Reduced interest and pleasure in activities you used to enjoy

- Intense irritability and anger

- Fear that you're not a good mother

- Hopelessness

- Feelings of worthlessness, shame, guilt, or inadequacy

- Diminished ability to think clearly, concentrate, or

make decisions

- Restlessness

- Severe anxiety and panic attacks

- Thoughts of harming yourself or your baby

- Recurrent thoughts of death or suicide

Untreated, postpartum depression may last for many months or longer.

Postpartum anxiety

According to Postpartum Support International, approximately six percent of pregnant women and ten percent of postpartum women develop anxiety. Sometimes they experience anxiety alone, and sometimes they experience it in addition to depression.

The symptoms of anxiety during pregnancy or postpartum might include:

- Constant worry

- Feeling that something bad is going to happen

- Racing thoughts

- Disturbances of sleep and appetite

- Inability to sit still

- Dizziness, hot flashes, and nausea

Risk factors for perinatal anxiety and panic include a personal or family history of anxiety, previous perinatal depression or anxiety, or thyroid imbalance.

In addition to generalized anxiety, there are some specific forms of anxiety that you should know about. One is **postpartum panic disorder**. This is a form of anxiety with which the sufferer feels very nervous and has recurring panic attacks. During a panic attack, she may experience shortness of breath, chest pain, claustrophobia, dizziness, heart palpitations, and numbness and tingling in the extremities. Panic attacks seem to go in waves, but it is important to know that they will pass and will not hurt you.

Another form of anxiety is **postpartum obsessive compulsive disorder.**

Postpartum and antepartum anxiety are temporary and treatable with professional help. If you feel you may be suffering from one of these illnesses, know that it is not your fault and you are not to blame. You can use our resource page to reach out now for help. We understand what you are going through and will connect you to people who understand and can help.

Postpartum obsessive compulsive disorder

According to Postpartum Support International, postpartum OCD is the most misunderstood and misdiagnosed of the perinatal disorders. You do not have to be diagnosed with OCD to experience these common symptoms of perinatal anxiety.

It is estimated that as many as three to five percent of new mothers and some new fathers will experience these symptoms. The repetitive, intrusive images and thoughts are very frightening and can feel like they come "out of the blue." **Research has shown that these images are anxious in nature, not delusional, and have very low risk of being acted upon**. It is far more likely that the parent with this symptom takes steps to avoid triggers and avoid what they fear is potentially harmful to the baby.

Symptoms of perinatal obsessive-compulsive disorder can include:

- Obsessions, also called intrusive thoughts, which are persistent repetitive thoughts or mental images related to the baby. These thoughts are very upsetting and not something the woman has ever experienced before.

- Compulsions, where the mom may do certain things over and over again to reduce her fears and obsessions. This may include needing to clean constantly, check things many times, or repeatedly count or reorder things.

- A sense of horror about these obsessions.

- Fear of being left alone with the infant.

- Hypervigilance in protecting the infant.

Moms with postpartum OCD know that their thoughts are bizarre, and they are very unlikely to ever act on them.

Risk factors for postpartum OCD include a personal or family history of anxiety or OCD.

Postpartum OCD is temporary and treatable with professional help. If you feel you may be suffering from this illness, know that it is not your fault and you are not to blame.

<u>Postpartum depression in new fathers.</u>

According to Postpartum Support International, new fathers can experience postpartum depression, too. They may experience anxiety, have changes in their usual eating and sleeping patterns, or feel sad, fatigued, or overwhelmed; the same symptoms mothers with postpartum depression experience.

Fathers who are young, have a history of depression, experience relationship problems, or are struggling financially are most at risk of postpartum depression. Postpartum depression in fathers - sometimes called paternal postpartum depression - can have the same negative effect on partner relationships and child development as postpartum depression in mothers can.

If you're a new father and are experiencing symptoms of depression or anxiety during your partner's pregnancy or in the first year after your child's birth, talk to a healthcare professional. Similar treatments and supports provided to mothers with postpartum depression can be beneficial in treating postpartum depression in fathers. See more for dads in chapter nine.

Commonalities in postpartum mood disorders

The number one commonality among postpartum mood disorders is, "something feels off." After childbirth, of course you don't feel like yourself. You just had a baby ram through your vagina (which now looks like a Mack truck ran through it), your boobs are enormous and achy, and you're more tired than you've ever been in your life. But this "off" feeling is in relation whatever is normal for you. If you're having a hard time finding that normal part of yourself, that's your first sign that something is off. I ignored it and said, "I'm just tired" for a year until I was finally diagnosed, but that should have been my first sign that I was in trouble. And because I lost that piece of my normal self nearly three years ago, it's been so hard to find it again and is something I'm still struggling with.

Another commonality is intrusive thoughts. Every new mom worries about taking a baby home the first time. Can you co-sleep? Are they still breathing in their little crib? Are they too hot in the swaddle? The questions and worries are non-stop. But do they elicit a panic? Are you doubting everything, including your gut instinct and your logical lizard brain telling you "everything is fine"? If so, you may be up against some postpartum depression or anxiety.

But most importantly, any of the above symptoms are cause for concern, and you should feel comfortable telling your partner about it so they can start keeping an eye on you. You should then call one of the resources at the start of this book and find a counselor in your area who can really help you through whatever it is you're feeling - even if it's not serious. Counseling never hurt anyone; think of it as preventative care.

Diagnosis

I mentioned it in the beginning, but I'll say again: it's recommended that OB/GYNs, midwives, and pediatricians all screen new moms for signs of postpartum mood disorders. Whether or not they do is up for debate and depends a lot on where you live, the age and training of your medical professionals, and ot her factors. In my experience and opinion, a lot of women are not being screened properly and are going undiagnosed for longer periods of time. An OB/GYN should be able to diagnose you properly, but if they're not trained to really understand the signs and symptoms, you're better off mentioning it to them and getting a recommendation or referral for a therapist/psychiatrist in your area who can diagnose and treat you effectively .You don't want to be bounced around from one provider to the next, because the quicker you can be diagnosed and start treatment, the quicker you can start to feel better. You know when something is wrong with you, and in this case it's 100 percent acceptable to call up a shrink and say, "Hey, I think I've got some postpartum depression or something going on, and I could use some help." It's better to ask for help than to wait for someone to give it to you.

**DISCLAIMER: This next part gets pretty dense but it's worth a read if you want to know all of your options, even if you're currently undergoing a treatment plan. The more you know... **

Treatment options

There is no one-size-fits-all treatment for these disorders. As you'll learn from the interviews later in this book, women have had different experiences, been diagnosed at different times, and have sought different treatments for their disorders. Everyone's hormones and brain chemistry are different. Some women respond well to medication, some need intensive therapy, group therapy, etc. You've got to find what works for you. It helps if you've got at least a counselor you can talk to who can also help you find the resources to get on the right track.

Fluoxetine
20mg daily
Setr
15,
Buspirone
10mg
as needed
Nortriptyline
15mg daily

The following is taken from an article published in the International Journal of Women's Health in 2011.

Pharmacological treatments for postpartum depression

Antidepressant medication

A small but growing literature suggests that postpartum depression can be thought of as a variant of major depression that responds similarly to antidepressant medication. Concerns unique to pharmacologic treatment of PPD include metabolic changes in the postpartum period, exposure of the infant to medication in breast milk, the effect of depression and treatment on the ability of the depressed mother to care for a new baby, and the perceived stigma of being seen as a "bad mother" for requiring medication. These factors, as well as the woman's level of distress, access to care, and experience with past treatment may influence the decision of the patient and her caregiver regarding the choice of pharmacologic and nonpharmacologic treatments for PPD.

Data comparing the effectiveness of medication against other treatment modalities for PPD are scarce, though do suggest that medications are at least as effective as most *psychological interventions based on effect size. To date, four[1] randomized controlled studies on the treatment of PPD with antidepressant medications have been published, along with several open trials. Additionally, two randomized studies have looked at the prevention of PPD with antidepressant medication.*

In a study of 87 women with major or minor depression in the postpartum period, subjects were randomized to one of four groups receiving either fluoxetine (Prozac) or placebo plus one or six cognitive behavioral therapy (CBT) based counseling sessions. Breastfeeding mothers were excluded from the study. Improvement was seen in all groups, with greater reduction in depression severity in the fluoxetine group compared to the placebo medication, and greater improvement with six counseling sessions compared to one session. Women receiving both fluoxetine and counseling did not differ significantly in outcome compared to women who received fluoxetine alone. Because the mean baseline level of depressive symptoms based on rating scales was mild, the findings are not easily generalized to a population with more severe postpartum depression.

---

[1] Only four!!

A subsequent study randomized 35 women with postpartum depression and comorbid anxiety to receive paroxetine or paroxetine plus CBT (cognitive behavioral therapy) for 12 weeks. Both groups showed significant improvement in depressive and anxiety symptoms (response rates 87.5 percent in the paroxetine (Paxil) group and 78.9 percent in the combined group) without significant differences between groups. The study did not include a placebo arm, making analysis of the specific effects of either intervention difficult. A third study compared paroxetine to placebo in an 8-week randomized controlled trial. The attrition rate in this study was high, with only 31 of 70 participants completing the study (17 in the paroxetine arm and 14 in the placebo arm), but the authors found lower mean severity scores and a higher remission rate after 8 weeks of treatment with paroxetine compared to placebo.

Very few studies have compared different classes of medications used in postpartum depression. *One comparative study found treatment with nortriptyline (Pamelor) to yield similar outcomes as treatment with sertraline (Zoloft). After eight weeks of treatment in this large, randomized, double-blind trial, both groups showed improvement, and response rates (nortriptyline 69 percent,* sertraline 56 percent), remission rates (nortriptyline 48 percent, sertraline 46 percent) and side effect burden were similar between groups at week 4, 8 and 24, though side effect profiles differed. There was no placebo arm. The response rate could be predicted earlier in the group receiving sertraline, but the overall response rates were equivalent. Sub-analyses of this study revealed an improvement in maternal role function and sexual function that was equivalent in both groups.

Several open studies have found sertraline, venlafaxine (Effexor), nefazodone, fluvoxamine, and bupropion to be effective in the treatment of postpartum depression. These studies have been small, with 4–15 participants, lacked control groups, and in several cases were sponsored by the pharmaceutical companies manufacturing the studied drug. Though there is little data comparing medications to placebo in the perinatal population, taken together, data from both the controlled and open studies suggest that antidepressants typically used to treat major depression are equally effective in postpartum depression, without clear differences between medications in efficacy and side effect burden. Therefore, some experts recommend that if a patient has responded to a specific antidepressant in the past, that medication should be among the first to be

"Two placebo-controlled studies have looked at the role of medication in preventing recurrent PPD. In one small, randomized placebo controlled pilot study, sertraline initiated shortly after birth for non-depressed women with at least one prior episode of PPD was found to prevent recurrence and prolong time to relapse. However, in another study, no difference was found in rates of recurrence or time to relapse between patients receiving nortriptyline and patients receiving placebo: one out of four women in both groups suffered a relapse within the 20 week study period. (Author's note: this was me.) Further research is needed to conclude whether initiation of antidepressants after childbirth in a select group of high risk women is preventative against postpartum depression."

considered in treating her depression in the postpartum.

Breastfeeding considerations

The benefits of breastfeeding have been well described and
have led the World Health Organization, the American
Academy of Pediatrics and the American Academy of
Family Practitioners to recommend breastfeeding for at
least the first six months for most women. Potential effects
of antidepressant medication on breastfeeding are of
concern to many mothers and clinicians.[2]

The report continues:

The long-term risks of low-level exposure to antidepressant
medication in breast milk are largely unknown. The risks
of untreated maternal depression are well-known and
significant. Some experts recommend that if medication
treatment is indicated, clinical factors such as the patient's
prior response or nonresponse to an individual medication
rather than data on blood levels should take precedence
in the choice of first-line agent. Decisions about initiating

____

[2]In my opinion, these concerns have led a lot of practitioners to steer
moms away from getting medication to help treat their mood disorders.

anti-depressant medication during breastfeeding and the choice of agent must be made on a case-by-case basis, and should involve a discussion of clinical factors, including severity of the depressive symptoms and prior response to medications and/or psychotherapy, known and unknown risks of the medication, the known risks of under- or untreated depression, and the patient's preferences. Regardless of which antidepressant medication a breastfeeding mother takes, the infant's pediatrician should be made aware of the possible exposure, and the infant should be monitored for changes in feeding patterns, sleeping patterns, sedation, irritability and other signs of drug toxicity. As blood levels have not been correlated with adverse effects, routine laboratory testing of infant blood levels is not currently recommended.

The above selection is taken from the following article:

Fitelson, Elizabeth; et al. Treatment of postpartum depression: clinical, psychological and pharmacological options. (Dec. 30, 2010). *International Journal of Women's Health*(3), 1-14. doi: 10.2147/IJWH.S6938.

A psychiatrist is not going to prescribe something that will hurt your baby. If there is even a slight risk to your baby, they won't put you on medication, or they'll put you on the lowest dose possible. But your health and your happiness are more important than breastfeeding for a year. I hate to break it to ya, but they are. There is no shame in formula-feeding your baby. Your baby is better off getting his or her nutrients from a bottle and having a healthy loving mother than having an emotionally distraught mother breastfeed them while just trying to keep it together to make it through another day. You have to put yourself first in order to take care of your child. You are the ship, and if you go down, the entire family goes down with you. (This was hard to hear from my therapists, but it was 100 percent what I needed to hear.)

Here's more from the article:

Hormone therapy

There is a dramatic drop in maternal levels of estrogen and progesterone at the time of delivery, and this shift has been proposed as one trigger for the onset of PPD in some women. Effects of estrogen in the brain include the promotion of neuronal growth and survival, enhancement of neurotransmitter activity, mitigation of oxidative stress and modulation of the hypophyseal-pituitary axis. A study designed to replicate the hormonal changes experienced around the time of birth found that women with a prior history of postpartum depression experienced mood symptoms when exposed to a drop in estradiol and progesterone, whereas women without a history of PPD did not. **This finding suggests vulnerability to hormone shifts in a subset of the population, and raises the possibility of hormonal intervention as a treatment or preventative intervention for PPD.**

In a double-blind placebo-controlled study by Gregoire et al 61 women with postpartum depression were randomized to receive estrogen or placebo patches. Breastfeeding women were excluded. Over the first month of treatment, women receiving estrogen showed greater and more rapid improvement in their symptoms as measured on the Edinburgh Postnatal Depression Scale and in clinical interviews. Women in the placebo group also improved, but maintained depression scores above the screening threshold. Neither group had complete remission of symptoms. The authors did not control for women receiving concomitant antidepressant medication, which was more common in the estrogen treatment group, making interpretation of the study results difficult. Additionally, women were included in the study up to 18 months postpartum, by which time the effects the postpartum drop in estrogen would likely have resolved.

Although an early naturalistic study suggested progesterone as a promising preventative therapy against recurrent postpartum depression, the results of that study were contradicted by a subsequent double-blind, placebo-controlled trial that found an increase in depressive symptoms in women treated with norethisterone enanthate, a synthetic progestogen. In this study, 180 women were randomized to receive one depot injection of norethisterone enanthate or one injection of saline placebo within 48 hours after delivery and were followed for three months. The investigators found that women who received the synthetic progestogen were more likely to develop depressive symptoms, more likely to have bleeding, and more likely to complain of exhaustion. A recent review of the above studies concluded that while the research on estrogen is promising but preliminary, there is no role for synthetic progestogens in the treatment of PPD, and that given the increased risk for depressive symptoms their use as contraception in this population is questionable.

Other studies without control groups support an effect of estrogen in the treatment of postpartum depression. A small prevention study found that when a slow taper of estrogen therapy was administered immediately after birth to 11 women with a history of postpartum psychosis or depression only one woman suffered a relapse episode. Another small study treated 23 women with severe postpartum depression with sublingual 17-beta estradiol over 8 weeks, and found remission of symptoms in 19 of the women, which the authors correlated with increased serum estrogen levels in the subjects. Both studies should be interpreted with caution, given the lack of a comparison group.

Although initial results for the use of estrogen in the treatment of postpartum depression are promising, additional methodologically sound studies are needed. Furthermore, estrogen therapy should not be used in women with an increased risk of thromboembolism. Treatment with gonadal steroids can interfere with lactation, which should be discussed with women prior to initiating therapy. Long-term use of estrogen therapy can cause endometrial hyperplasia and slightly elevates the risk of endometrial cancer; although this risk can be mitigated by co-administration of progesterone, the increase in depressive symptoms with progestogen seen in the Lawrie study complicates the implementation of this strategy.

Psychological and psychosocial treatments for postpartum depression

Many mothers with postpartum depression are hesitant to take antidepressants due to concerns about infant exposure to medication through breast milk or concerns about potential side effects, and therefore often prefer psychological treatments. Although relatively few studies have systematically investigated nonpharmacologic treatments for PPD, existing research supports the use of both psychological treatments (specifically interpersonal therapy, cognitive-behavioral therapy, and psychodynamic psychotherapy), as well as psychosocial interventions, such as nondirective counseling. A Cochrane meta-analysis of ten randomized controlled trials of psychosocial and psychological treatments for postpartum depression concluded that both psychosocial and psychological interventions are effective in decreasing depression and are viable treatment options for postpartum depression.

Interpersonal therapy (IPT)

Interpersonal therapy (IPT) is a time-limited treatment for major depression based on addressing the connection between interpersonal problems and mood, which frames depression as a medical illness occurring in a social context. In IPT, the patient and clinician select one of four interpersonal problem areas (role transition, role dispute, grief, or interpersonal deficits) as a treatment focus. Over the course of the therapy (typically 12–20 weeks), strategies are pursued to assist patients in modifying problematic approaches to relationships and in building better social supports. IPT has been adapted to address problem areas relevant to postpartum depression such as the relationship between mother and infant, mother and partner, and transition back to work. The fact that IPT is both time-limited and problem-focused fits well with the demands of the postpartum mother.

Several studies, including one large-scale randomized controlled trial, have supported the effectiveness of IPT for treating postpartum depression. O'Hara and colleagues randomized 120 women with postpartum depression to receive 12 weekly 60-minute individual sessions of manualized IPT by a trained therapist versus control condition of a wait-list. The women who received IPT had a significant decrease in their depressive symptomatology (measured by Hamilton Depression Rating Scale and Beck Depression Inventory) as compared to the wait-list group, as well as significant improvement in social adjustment scores. In another study by Clark et al 35 women with postpartum depression were assigned to individual IPT (12 sessions) versus mother-infant group therapy versus a wait-list condition. Both IPT and mother-infant group therapy were associated with greater reduction in depressive symptoms as compared to the wait-list conditions. Both studies support the effectiveness of IPT as a treatment for PPD, though there is not enough data to suggest a specific benefit to IPT compared with other therapeutic modalities.

Two small open studies have evaluated group IPT for postpartum depression. Klier et al conducted a pilot study in which 17 depressed women in two different groups received 9 weeks of group IPT and 3 individual sessions. Depression scores on two rating scales decreased significantly during the course of treatment, and gains were maintained at 6-month follow-up. However, there was a high attrition rate (6 out of 17), and the study was also limited by small sample size, lack of a control group, and lack of an independent rater. Similarly, Reay et al treated, in an open pilot trial, 18 women diagnosed with postpartum depression with 8 group IPT sessions, as well as two individual and one partner session. Depressive symptoms decreased significantly, and these gains were maintained at three months. Compared to the previous study, the drop-out rate was low, and authors speculated that this might be due to childcare provided. However, two-thirds of the study participants were receiving antidepressant therapy concomitantly, limiting interpretation of the effect of this group intervention. While it is difficult to make conclusions about efficacy based on this pilot data, the study authors suggest that advantages to group over individual IPT for postpartum depression might include increased social support, normalization of problems, development of interpersonal skills in a group setting that can be translated to outside relationships, and minimization of stigma associated with PPD.

Cognitive behavioral therapy (CBT)

Cognitive behavioral therapy (CBT), a well-studied and effective treatment for major depression, is based on the premise that both perceptions and behaviors are intimately linked to mood. CBT focuses on helping depressed patients to modify distorted patterns of negative thinking and to make behavioral changes that enhance coping and reduce distress. There have been several trials assessing CBT alone or with other interventions for the treatment of PPD. In a randomized controlled psychotherapy-pharmacotherapy study, Appleby et al assigned 87 women with PPD to one of four conditions in a factorial design, varying based on treatment with either one or six sessions of CBT-based counseling, and treatment with fluoxetine or placebo. All four treatment groups had significant improvement in depressive symptoms. Women who received six CBT sessions versus one had greater decrease in depressive symptoms. Six sessions of CBT plus placebo pill was as effective as treatment with fluoxetine plus one session of CBT, but there was no added benefit in the group receiving 6 counseling sessions in combination with fluoxetine. It should be noted that the counseling sessions were delivered by briefly trained nonspecialists, and six sessions of CBT may not be a sufficient representation of a standard course of treatment.

In another combination medication-CBT study, Misri et al randomized 35 women with PPD and comorbid anxiety either to paroxetine monotherapy or paroxetine and 12 weekly manualized CBT sessions with a psychologist. While both groups had significant decreases in depressive symptoms, there were no significant differences between the two groups in response rates, time to remission or dose of medication required, suggesting no measurable added benefit to the CBT treatment in combination with an SSRI over the 12 week study period, as consistent with Appleby's findings. In a randomized controlled trial looking at the effectiveness of CBT versus a control condition, Prendergast and Austin assigned 37 women with PPD either to six weekly one-hour home-based CBT sessions delivered by early childhood nurses (ECNs) or to "ideal standard care", which consisted of six weekly visits to ECNs in a clinic setting. Both groups with PPD had significant mood improvement, though there was a non-significant trend towards CBT being more effective at six-month follow-up. Among study limitations, ECNs administering CBT were not experienced therapists, though they received CBT training prior to the study and supervision throughout. Additionally, the control group more closely resembled a supportive psychotherapy rather than no treatment. These studies support CBT interventions as helpful in the treatment of PPD, though they do not support an additional benefit to CBT in combination with pharmacotherapy and do not clarify a specific benefit of CBT for this population in comparison with other treatments. Two of these studies also suggest a role for the training of non-mental-health professionals in this modality.

Nondirective counseling

As compared with IPT or CBT, psychosocial interventions are unstructured and non-manualized, and include nondirective counseling and peer support. Nondirective counseling (also known as "person-centered") is based on the use of empathic and nonjudgmental listening and support. In the first notable study evaluating this intervention, Holden randomized 50 women with PPD to 8 weekly nondirective counseling sessions with a health visitor or routine primary care. A health visitor in the UK is a public health nurse who conducts home visits with pregnant and postpartum women. This study found that the rate of recovery from PPD for counseling (69 percent) was significantly greater than that of the control group (38 percent). In a similar study conducted in Sweden, Wickberg and Hwang randomized 31 women with PPD to receive six nondirective counseling sessions by child health clinic nurses or routine primary care.

As in the Holden study, a significantly greater percentage of women in the treatment group (80 percent) had remission of depression than in the control group (25 percent). Study limitations include the removal of four study participants, two in each group, for more intensive mental health services due to illness severity.

Peer and partner support

Epidemiologic data as well as some prospective studies have consistently identified inadequate social support as a risk factor for developing postpartum depression, thus raising the possibility of interventions aimed at increasing social supports as treatment options for perinatal depression. In a prospective cohort of pregnant Chinese women, Xie et al found that low support in both the prenatal and postnatal time period was associated with increased risk for postpartum depression, with the highest risk for postpartum women who had low objective or practical support. The broad applicability of this study is limited by the demographics of its cohort (limited to married Chinese primiparous women without significant obstetric complications, rates of Caesarian delivery over 70 percent) and the use of a rating scale most validated in the Chinese population. However, the finding suggests *that tangible social support, such as assistance with caring for the newborn, may be particularly important and helpful in the treatment of postpartum depressed mothers.*

In a pilot study, CL Dennis evaluated the effect of mother-to-mother support as delivered over the telephone on depressive symptomatology in a postpartum patient population identified as at high risk for PPD based on EPDS score >9. Standard postpartum care in addition to individualized telephone-based peer support resulted in a significant reduction in depressive symptoms at 8 weeks. More recently, in a larger randomized multisite trial, Dennis and colleagues demonstrated that high-risk postpartum women who received telephone-based peer support over 12 weeks were at lower risk for developing PPD (as defined by EPDS >12) compared to a control group receiving usual care. Due in part to the telephone-based nature of the study, the investigators were unable to confirm the findings from rating scales with structured clinical interviews.

While poor partner support has been identified as an important risk factor for PPD, few studies have investigated the role of the partner or other family support in recovery from PPD. In one survey study, shared activities, problem-focused information and assistance, and positive feedback from the partner decreased a mother's likelihood of having depressive symptoms at 8 weeks postpartum. A qualitative study examining factors identified by women who had recovered from PPD to be most important in their recovery found that "emotional support from partner", "improved communication with partner", "practical support from partner", and "emotional support from friends" were rated as "essential" to recovery. A small, nonblinded study by Misri et al examined the impact of partner support in the treatment of PPD. In this study, 29 women with PPD were randomized to receive 7 sessions of psychoeducation with (support arm) or without (control arm) their partners. Relative to the control group, women in the partner group had significant reductions in depressive symptoms, while the partners in this group may also have had protective benefit on measures of general health. These studies do not provide enough data to recommend a specific partner-based intervention, but they do suggest that including the partner in the treatment of PPD may be of benefit for some women.

Comparisons of psychological and psychosocial treatments

Cooper et al designed a large study to assess the effects of different psychological interventions on PPD. A community sample of 193 women with PPD were randomized to receive from weeks 8-18 postpartum routine primary

care versus one of three treatment conditions: CBT,
psychodynamic psychotherapy, or nondirective counseling.
All three treatments decreased depressive symptoms
significantly as measured by EPDS at 4.5 months, in
comparison to no treatment. Rates of remission from
depression, as defined by DSM-III, were higher for
those receiving psychodynamic therapy (71 percent)
than CBT (57 percent) or nondirective counseling (54
percent). However, there were no differences among
any of the groups at the 9 month assessment. Milgrom
et al also undertook a study to compare different
psychological interventions for PPD. A community of 192
women with PPD were randomized to routine primary
care or 12 weeks of group-based CBT, or group-based
or individual counseling utilizing supportive therapy
techniques delivered by trained therapists. All three
psychological interventions were superior to routine
care in reducing symptoms of PPD. While there were
no significant differences between counseling and
CBT, individual counseling was slightly more effective
than group counseling. Finally, Morrell et al in a large,
cluster randomized trial, looked at an intervention that
trained health visitors to identify depressive symptoms
in postnatal women and to deliver either a cognitive
behavioral or nondirective "person-centered" approach

involving up to eight sessions of individual counseling. They compared this with usual care delivered by health visitors who did not receive this training, in conjunction with general practitioners. In this study, women who had an EPDS score $\geq$12 at 6 weeks postpartum were followed for 18 months. At 6 months, significantly more women in the control condition remained with elevated EPDS scores compared to both intervention groups, and the differences persisted at 12 months. There were no differences between the two counseling approaches. While the specific effective component of the intervention was unclear, this study does provide evidence that training in psychologically-informed approaches for non mental-health providers can significantly enhance the care of depressed postnatal women.

A recent meta-analysis compared psychological and psychosocial interventions for PPD, including CBT, IPT, and nondirective counseling, as well as peer support. This study did not find any difference in effect size for any of these treatments, and concluded that different types of psychological interventions seem equally effective for treatment of PPD.

In summary, both psychological and psychosocial interventions for PPD have shown benefit over no treatment or "usual

<u>care" in multiple studies.</u> Further studies are needed to discriminate between the effectiveness of various psychological and psychosocial treatments for PPD and between group-based and individual modalities.

Other nonpharmacologic treatments for postpartum depression

Many women suffering from PPD and their healthcare providers may seek alternatives or adjuncts to standard psychological or pharmacologic treatments because of their concern about the effects of pharmacological treatment on breastfeeding, access to care, issues of stigma in the treatment of mental illness, limited effectiveness, or personal beliefs. In the following we have provided an overview of a variety of evidence-based nonpharmacologic treatments for postpartum depression.

Electroconvulsive therapy

As with treatment-refractory major depression in the general population, electroconvulsive therapy (ECT) is an option for depressed postpartum women who do not respond to antidepressant medication or who have severe or psychotic symptoms. Data specific to this population are very limited. One small study of five women receiving

ECT for refractory postpartum depression reported a 100 percent remission rate. Apart from concerns regarding anesthesia and breastfeeding, the use of ECT for postpartum depression does not differ from its use in major depression. Anesthetic agents used in ECT are typically rapidly metabolized, and risk of transmission in breast milk can be minimized by timing breastfeeding accordingly.

Bright light therapy

While bright light therapy was initially introduced as a treatment for seasonal affective disorder, research has supported its effectiveness as a treatment for nonseasonal depression. Light therapy presents an attractive option for the treatment of perinatal depression, as there are no known risks to the fetus or nursing infant. However, despite some encouraging preliminary data in antenatal depression, there is currently insufficient data on its effectiveness in the postpartum population. In one study, 15 outpatient women with PPD were randomly assigned to receive bright light (10,000 lux, $n = 10$) or dim red light (600 lux, $n = 5$) daily for six weeks. This study was unable to elicit a specific treatment effect of the light therapy due to the small sample size, though both groups showed significant improvement over time on all measures of depression. Further studies are required to clarify the effectiveness of light therapy in the treatment of postpartum depression.[3]

Omega-3 fatty acids

Omega-3 fatty acids have received specific attention in the treatment of perinatal depression, because of the known health benefits of these compounds for pregnant and postpartum women as well as some data showing positive effects on mood in the general population. Omega-3 fatty acids such as the eicosapentaenoic acid (EPA) and docosa-hexaenoic acid (DHA) found in fish oils, are the key building blocks for the development of a baby's central nervous system while in utero, and depletion of maternal omega-3 fatty acids occurs during pregnancy to facilitate this process. One often-cited cross-national study evaluating major depression in the general population demonstrated that per capita fish consumption was inversely related to the risk of developing major

[3]You can buy these therapeutic bright lights on Amazon. They're not cheap (about $200), and it's heads or tails as to if they work. I've got one. I use it sometimes if the weather is really bad, but normally I just try and make sure I've got all the blinds open to let the sun in and I get out for walks when I can. But we live in Texas, and it's always hot and sunny here. If you're in the northwest, northeast, or Canada, maybe consider one. It can't hurt.

depression. Further epidemiologic data support an association between low omega-3 intake from seafood and increased risk of high levels of depressive symptoms during pregnancy.

Despite these epidemiologic associations, studies examining the use of omega-3 fatty acids for treatment of perinatal depression have had mixed results. Freeman et al conducted two pilot studies of omega-3 fatty acids as an intervention for perinatal depression; one was an open-label flexible-dose trial of a combination of EPA and DHA for the treatment of MDD during pregnancy, and the second trial assessed the efficacy of omega-3 fatty acids for postpartum depression in an 8-week randomized dose-ranging study.The outcome of the first trial showed a 40.9 percent mean decrease in depressive symptoms on the Edinburgh Postnatal Depression Scale. The second study, a randomized dose-ranging trial for postpartum depression found no significant difference between control and study group. Both studies were limited by their small sample sizes (n = 15 and 16, respectively) and their lack of a placebo group. A subsequent randomized placebo-controlled study investigating the combination of omega-3 fatty acids and supportive psychotherapy for the treatment of perinatal depression again demonstrated no significant difference between the omega-3 fatty acids and placebo, though participants in both groups experienced significant decreases in their depression rating scales. The benefits of supportive psychotherapy received by both groups may have limited the ability to detect a specific effect of omega-3 fatty acids. A subsequent small, randomized, double blind, placebo-controlled trial investigating omega-3 fatty acids at a dose of 3.4 g per day as monotherapy for major depression during pregnancy demonstrated a benefit from this intervention. Although there was relatively high attrition in both groups, subjects receiving omega-3 fatty acids had significantly lower scores on depression rating scales as compared to the placebo group at the study end point.

In sum, omega-3 fatty acids may have therapeutic benefits for perinatal depression, but thus far most studies investigating this effect have been limited by small sample sizes. Some of these studies did establish that dietary intake of omega-3 fatty acids among participants was low prior to study involvement. Omega-3 fatty acids have clear health advantages for both the mother and for the developing fetus or nursing infant. Of note, omega-3 fatty acids can increase bleeding times at high doses, but according to a recent study, omega-3s at doses of 3-4 g per day produced no clinically significant increase in bleeding times or in bleeding events in patients with cardiovascular disease already treated with anti-platelet agents.

Acupuncture and massage

Acupuncture is the ancient Chinese tradition of the inserting and manipulating needles into various points on the body to treat pathologic processes and relieve pain. It has been investigated for the treatment of depression in the general population with mixed results, and has been increasingly investigated as adjunctive treatment in pregnancy for nausea, pain, breech presentation and induction of labor. There is no data about the use of acupuncture in postnatal depression, but one small pilot study by Manber et al compared the effectiveness of targeted acupuncture vs controls of a nontargeted acupuncture and massage in the treatment of pregnant depressed women eight weeks of an active acupuncture intervention targeted specifically for depression (treatments were standardized but individually tailored) significantly outperformed a massage intervention in terms of reduction of depressive symptom rating scales in depressed pregnant women.

While there was no significant difference in symptom reduction between the targeted and control acupuncture treatments in this study, a more recently published larger randomized trial of acupuncture in pregnant women showed significant reduction in depressive symptoms in active treatment versus both control conditions. The authors caution that the study was not designed to assess the effectiveness of massage as a treatment for perinatal depression. It is not clear what the effects of antenatal or postnatal acupuncture are on postnatal depression. It should be noted that as acupuncture may have effects on induction of labor and lactation, women who wish to try acupuncture as a treatment or adjunctive therapy for perinatal depression should be sure the practitioner is experienced in these issues.

Massage as treatment for perinatal depression has also been examined independently, and modalities include therapeutic massage, partner-delivered massage, and instruction in infant-massage in the postpartum period. Field et al looked at the effect of 10 sessions of massage versus 10 sessions of relaxation techniques in 32 adolescent inpatients with postnatal depression, and found a significant improvement in depression ratings in the massage group after session 10 but not the relaxation group. There was no longer-term follow up, so the clinical implications of this study are limited. Another study looked at the effects of infant massage, and compared the effects of 15 minutes of rocking versus 15 minutes of massage on 40 full-term infants between the ages of 1- and 3-months born to depressed mothers. They found multiple benefits for the infants in the massage group, including improvements in sleep patterns, interactions, crying, weight gain, and lower cortisol levels, though there was no measure of effects on maternal depression. Onozawa et al compared outcomes in mother–infant pairs who received five weekly sessions of infant massage classes plus a support group with mothers who were in a support group alone. Depression scores in both groups decreased without significant difference, but only the infant massage group showed statistically significant improvement in global ratings of mother–infant interactions. However, there was high drop-out in this study, and significant improvement in the massage group occurred prior to the first class, suggesting nonspecific or anticipatory benefit. A subsequent trial with a similar design failed to demonstrate these same advantages in mother–infant interactions after six sessions of infant massage compared to support groups alone, and depression scores in both groups again improved similarly.

A more recent study investigated maternal massage therapy administered by the woman's partner for 12 weeks in depressed pregnant women and found benefit in the massage group on indices of depression during late pregnancy and immediately postpartum, as well as lower cortisol levels in mothers and neonates. However, the control condition was unspecified standard care, and as there was no longer term follow-up the impact of the intervention on PPD is unclear. In summary, massage in its various forms described above has few risks, and may have benefits for women and their infants, but its effectiveness as a treatment for PPD remains in question.

Exercise

Several studies have investigated the role that exercise can play in alleviating postpartum depressive symptoms. A study by Da Costa et al looked at 88 women with PPD who were randomized to a 12-week, home-based exercise program or usual care. There was a reduction in depression rating scales in the intervention group as compared to the usual care group post-treatment, though not at the 3-month follow-up. However, Ko et al investigated a low-intensity exercise program that was specifically designed and administered to women with postpartum fatigue and *depression. There was no significant change in depression between the treatment group and the control group. Despite the limited evidence of efficacy for treatment of PPD, the UK National Institute for Health and Clinical Excellence (NICE) has recommended in their antenatal and postnatal mental health guidelines that health professionals should consider exercise as a management strategy in women experiencing mild-to-moderate depression. A review of the effects of exercise on PPD defined "feasible and effective" exercise as: moderate-intensity activities for at least 30 minutes per day, five days of the week, including walking in the form of "pram pushing."*

Exercise is helpful in life postpartum; not because you need to "get your body back," but because you need to get outside, get out of the house and cacophony of baby noises (even if the baby is with you), and you just need a chance to feel human again and get those endorphins pumping. Exercise gives you time to think about stuff while enjoying some fresh air. And if the weather is bad or you're tired, just do some pushups, a couple burpees, or some yoga moves. Just get your body moving for no other reason than to move. Get yourself out of your current frame of mind, your current funk, and your current position on the couch with the breastfeeding or bottle-feeding baby or manic toddler. Let them watch sesame street, put your headphones on, and just do something for you (more on this in a later chapter.)

There is no one-size-fits-all treatment for postpartum mood disorders, but we have come a long way. There are a lot of things you can try to find that work for you. While that is frustrating, please see the next image to see how far we've come in treating these disorders. It's only been in the last few decades that doctors have actually taken postpartum mood disorders seriously and differentiated between them and other psychological disorders. In another 10-20 years, hopefully the struggle won't be quite as bad.

The HISTORY of Postpartum Mood Disorders Diagnoses

*Info from 'Sadness and Support: A Short History of Postpartum Depression.'

4th Century

Hippocrates makes first known reference to PPD, stating cause was suppression of lochia + blood in the breasts. Referred to it as 'mania' and 'madness.'

13th Century

Tortula, female physician believed PPD was cause of mositure in body after childbirth.

"If the womb is too moist, the brain is filled with water, and the moisture running over the eyes compels them to involuntarily shed tears."

MIDDLE AGES

Women who exhibited 'melancholy' during or after childbirth were thought to be witches or victims of witchcraft.

16th Century

'Disturbances of the maternal instinct' focused on moms who kill their children – 'Melancholic filicide'. Led to study of postpartum disorders.

19th Century

Jean-Etienne Esquirol says PPD/ psychosis is either
peurperal: ocurs with first 6 wks
or
lactational: after 6 weeks
But no scientific basis for it. Treatments inclued warm baths, opium, restraints + separation from infants + family.

20th Century

Several scientists claimed postpartum disorders no different than dementia praecox, manic depression + delirium and petitioned AMA + APA to remove it from diagnostic manuals.

Two Freudian scientists said it was result of frigid personalities, supressed homosexuality + unresolved oedipal longings for their fathers.

Post WWII

It was noted women weren't seeking care for fear of being commited and separated from their children.

British + Australian psych wards developed to accomodate mothers and children so mothers could receive care.

1968

Brice Pitt describes 'atypical depression' in postpartum – acknowledging depression different from psychosis.

Pitt conducts first community-based study of PPD and found 10.8% of women had the disorder.

1994

PPD finally officially recognized in the Diagnostic Statistical Manual.

2006

Brooke Shields publishes 'Down Came The Rain', making PPD part of the national conversation in the US.

2010's

lots of research being done + universal screening recommended...

TBD

Chapter 5:

Where to go for help and what to look for in a therapist

The best way to find a therapist in your area who is equipped to deal with postpartum mood disorders is to utilize the guide in this book and the coordinators who are trained through Postpartum Support International (PSI). You can do this online, or by calling PSI at 1-800-944-4773.

As of September 2019, there's also a National Perinatal Mental Health Directory, put together by Postpartum Support International. It puts all of the perinatal health providers in your area at your fingertips. To learn more, visit https://directorypsichapters.com/.

Another way to find help is to ask your OB/GYN, midwife, doula, or general practitioner. Most will have no problem recommending a doctor who is equipped to handle your needs. But if money is an issue, make sure they know, so they can help you find someone who is in network, accepts insurance, or has payment plan options for patients who are self-pay. You may also be able to find a free option through a local organization. You can also contact your insurance company online or on the phone to find out what practitioners are covered. One way to make sure you're getting all your needs met is to contact a PSI coordinator who will have all of those options already put together for you so you won't get overwhelmed trying to find someone. We all know asking for help and then going out and looking for it is sometimes overwhelming, and it can hinder you from getting help.

Once you find a therapist, here are some questions to ask them directly, or at least ask yourself after that first meeting. And please remember, just because your first therapist might not be a good fit, it doesn't mean you won't find one who is a good fit. You don't have to settle for anyone you don't feel good about.

Questions to ask your therapist

- What are their experiences with postpartum women?

- What are their credentials?

- Have they ever received any training with postpartum depression in particular?

- What kind of approach to they take? Does this sound like something that will work for you?

- What do they think a treatment plan would look like for you based on the initial meeting? Does that make you feel good?

- Do you feel supported?

- Do you feel heard?

- Is it affordable? (If not, is it worth the expense for you and your family, or is it worth finding someone more affordable?)

- Are they flexible with their scheduling? If you're sick or your kid is sick, can you do your sessions over the phone?

- Are they OK with your kids coming with you when you can't get a sitter?

There are a couple of apps/virtual therapy options for those who really can't make the time to get to see one in-person, though I can't vouch for how well these services work. I've heard of TalkSpace and BetterHelp.com. You've just got to make sure that the therapist you're matched up with meets your needs, and you should change to a new therapist if not.

And, if you're feeling desperate and suicidal, please use the crisis help lines listed at the start of this book.

An interview with Abby Burd

Abby Burd is a Licensed Clinical Social Worker (LCSW) who has a private perinatal mental health practice in San Diego, California. She specializes in postpartum mental health and has developed an online class for pregnant women that helps prep them for life postpartum and helps ease the symptoms and length of postpartum depression/anxiety.

"I'm a mom of two. My girls are about to turn six and eight. I have worked in the mental health field since I was in college, so it's now 20-plus years I've been in the field," Burd said. "Even though it's what I do and I'm surrounded by it, I have experienced depression and anxiety in the past. It hadn't even clicked with me that that was the most common complication of childbirth. No one asked me, no one screened me. The OB just said 'see you in six weeks.'"

"I had physical complications (which I had no idea weren't normal) that no one was seeing me for. At that point, I don't think I met the criteria for postpartum depression

- but it did hit me like a ton of bricks. Breastfeeding had me crying; I just was not prepared. That was my experience with the first."

"My experience with my second was different for a lot of reasons. It was positive, and my birth was better. It made me keep wanting to have babies, have home births, be a doula, and help other moms have this experience. When I was about ten days postpartum (maybe two weeks), I was on the phone with a friend. My friend was approaching 42 weeks pregnant and really anxious. I remember being on the playground, wearing my baby, pushing my toddler, and talking to her about things she can do to reduce her anxiety that she already knew how to do. I was just basically encouraging her and helping her with her mindset. That was around lunchtime, and she had the baby before bedtime."

"That was when I realized I already had the skillset to help people with this, so I don't need to be a doula or change my discipline. I can bring my discipline to this area."

Burd said the big thing with postpartum mental health care is seeing the difference in women when they're supported and when they're not. Support is what makes the difference. When I told her my story, she said, "It sounds like you were doing everything right the second time, and it still hit you."

I originally reached out to Burd because her website is called "preventppd.com" and I kind of took it personally. Like, hadn't I done enough to not get it the second time around? How could she make this claim?

"So what I'm saying is not that we can totally prevent it. I wish we could prevent it, but we can reduce the likelihood. It sounds like you were doing many of the things I would recommend, and it still hit you. It just means you're one of the lucky ones that's in that section."

"After my second was born (while I was on maternity leave from where I was counselor for a college counseling center), I started my private practice geared toward perinatal mental health. It's been rewarding, and I've found a wonderful community of providers and allied professionals. I initially started off treating PPD/anxiety, perinatal loss, fertility, miscarriage, anxiety during pregnancy after loss, and relationships postpartum. It naturally happened that some of my clients said, 'I'm pregnant again or want to be, and what can I do to prevent post partum depression?'"

"Sometimes people do still have symptoms, but I feel for almost
     all of my clients it wasn't as severe or as bad the second
     time around, and they had a better experience. They
     asked for help sooner and got better sooner. I did have
     people reach out to me for therapy as a preventative
     measure during pregnancy or while they were trying
     to conceive. Or I was treating folks for anxiety and
     depression who were of childbearing age, so that's why
     we started working on prevention strategies for them."

"That's why I feel like prevention can be helpful."

"What is exciting to me is research that came out earlier this
     year (2019) from the U.S. Preventive Services Taskforce
     (the ones that recommended universal screenings for
     depression and postpartum depression). They looked
     at particular women at increased risk for perinatal
     depression. They also looked at lot of different
     modalities, medication, nutrition, diet, exercise, social
     support, and two different counseling methods - CBT
     (cognitive behavioral therapy) and IPT (interpersonal
     psychotherapy) - to find ways they could not just treat
     but prevent symptoms, specifically for women at an
     increased risk. The only two methods that showed an
     effect were these two counseling methods." (The same two

Burd currently uses with her patients.)

"So basically, the idea is using some of the same ways we have
for treating it as methods of prevention. Some of the
things I'll do in individual practice at the beginning of the
third trimester is have the partner come in and talk about
a postpartum plan for support, childcare, etc. I discuss
with the partner, 'How will you know she's at risk? Make
sure she's safe from suicide. How do we know when you'll
reach out for immediate help?' It could be individual for
each family."

"The idea is that it's like filling up the toolbox. For some,
it's awareness; some have no idea how post partum
depression can impact them. IPT is really good for that. It
looks at role transition, grief and loss, and interpersonal
relationships - and all of those are affected. It is one of
the most studied ways for treating postpartum mood
disorders. It's starting a conversation about, 'How is my
life going to change?'"

"If I meet someone all put together and two weeks postpartum,
that's a red flag to me that they're going to be really
hard on themselves. For type A personalities, what is
it going to be like to be a novice in a job that's 24/7,

grueling, boring, and not very validating?"

"It affects so many of us. Like I said, even if I didn't have clinical depression, I get it because it is a spectrum."

"The online course is not in any way a substitute for psychotherapy. One in five women are going to have a postpartum mood disorder, and at least three more are going to feel like they've been hit with a ton of bricks. Maybe for those three, this course will help them have a better transition to parenthood."

"And then for maybe the other one in five, there are still so many barriers to treatment. In my private practice, people contacted me and couldn't afford the fee, or they couldn't find a perinatal specialist within their insurance network, or they couldn't find childcare to come see me; there are a lot of logistical barriers. So I felt like this course could be an option for them, to be a jump start. Part of it is education. I wanted to be able to bring the stuff I felt helped the majority of people I see, and bring it to a wider audience."

Burd said her online class is mostly videos and blogs she's written over the years. She also includes journal prompts and provides a space within the course for mothers to speak with each other and provide peer-to-peer support.

Burd says interest in the course is growing, but she'd like to see more. And she's also working on creating a continuing education course for providers all about postpartum mood disorders and how to effectively treat patients.

And just because you're already postpartum and facing this doesn't mean Burd's course can't help you.

"There's a big section of my course on the reproductive story. It comes from a narrative therapy style where you're looking at the kind of the idea we've had in our head about, 'I always thought when I was a little girl I'd get married and have two or three kids. No one said I'd have four miscarriages, failed IVF rounds, massive hemorrhaging, or a NICU baby.' No one plans that, so when there's any kind of variance from the reproductive story, it's compounded loss. It's a disenfranchised grief we can't talk about and share. The reproductive story is maybe even more helpful for women who are already postpartum."

Burd said there's been a lot of progress in the care of postpartum women, but there needs to be more.

"In all of my clinical training - like graduate school, clinical internships, and afterwards, when I got to train at the University of California in San Diego along with the psychiatry residents - I don't even remember it (PPD) being mentioned. Now it's starting to change. I think perhaps we could look at misogyny as a culprit, but now women are the doctors, and maybe now it's starting to come out. I think women are starting to become more aware, but we need more providers. I happen to live in a town that has the San Diego Postpartum Alliance, which has been providing education for decades. But most people don't live in a city like this, so there's more needed for sure."

"I want women to have hope. I want them to know that this is common. But I don't want to say it's normal. PPD/A is so common, but we can make it better. It's not normal - like you don't have to put up with it. I want women to know that they have to prioritize themselves in order to take care of their children. It's not weakness to ask for help. Think about the CEO of a company. Does a CEO do everything themselves or do they delegate and know when to bring in a consultant? A therapist is a consultant."

Chapter 6:

The importance of getting help and what can happen if you don't

Welcome
to
MOTHERHOOD
'It takes a village'

Before you read the below section, please know I am not trying to guilt you into therapy. I'm not trying to make you feel bad about what you're going through, and I'm not trying to add to your stress or pressure. I just want you to be as informed as possible.

When you were pregnant, you probably Googled every toy, diaper, formula, and baby bottle. You probably read "What to Expect When You're Expecting," "The Wonder Weeks," and god knows what other parenting book out there, and this should be no different.

As a mother and a patient, it's important to be informed. It's good to know the details about your illness. It helps you wrap your head around things. There's nothing scarier than the unknown, and it helps when you know exactly what you're facing. That could make it scarier, but it shouldn't. Knowledge is power, and the better equipped we are with this knowledge, the better we can take care of ourselves and our kids.

As you read the following, just remember, YOU'VE GOT THIS. You're doing a good job. Just by picking up this book, you've taken a step in the right direction.

In the report from the International Journal of Women's Health that I quote in chapter four of this book, the authors write that therapeutic treatment of postpartum depression is important not only for the mother's health, but for the child's development.

Untreated maternal depression is associated with serious morbidity for the mother, the infant, and the family system. Perinatal depression causes significant suffering in women at a time when personal or societal notions of motherhood as a uniquely joyful, if tiring, experience may be incongruous with the depressed woman's ability to feel gratification in the mothering role, connect with her infant, or carry out the often overwhelming tasks of caring for a new baby.

Such a disconnect can reinforce the disabling sense of isolation, guilt, helplessness and hopelessness that frequently characterize the depressed state. Women with PPD are at higher risk for smoking, alcohol or illicit substance abuse, and are more likely than non-depressed mothers to experience current or recent physical, emotional, or sexual abuse. Although rates of suicide for women during pregnancy and the puerperum (less than six weeks postpartum) are lower than the general population, suicide is an important cause of maternal mortality. Self-inflicted injury is the leading cause of one-year maternal mortality in the United Kingdom. A recent World Health Organization report on women's health identifies self-inflicted injury as the second leading cause of maternal mortality in high-income countries; suicide remains an important cause of maternal deaths in moderate and low-income countries. Intrusive thoughts of accidental or intentional harm to the baby are common in the early postpartum time. These thoughts are more frequent and distressing in women with postpartum depression; however, nonpsychotic depressed women are unlikely to commit infanticide.

The adverse impact of maternal depression on infant outcomes has also been studied. Depression has significant negative effects on a mother's ability to interact appropriately with her child. Depressed women have been found to have poorer responsiveness to infant cues and more negative, hostile or disengaged parenting behaviors. These disruptions in maternal-infant interactions have been associated with lower cognitive functioning and adverse emotional development in children, and they appear to be universal across cultural and economic divides. Other parenting behaviors are also affected, including problematic sleep habits, lower preventative healthcare utilization and undesirable safety practices. Chronic depression in mothers places children at higher risk for behavioral problems and later psychopathology, including anxiety, disruptive, and affective disorders; conversely, remission of depression in mothers is associated with reduction or remission in the children's psychiatric diagnoses. Maternal depression also increases the risk for negative infant feeding outcomes, including lower rates of initiating or maintaining breastfeeding, lower levels of breastfeeding self-efficacy, and more difficulties while breastfeeding."

All of that is to say: GET HELP. Explore the various treatment options, find one that will work for you, and get help. You can't pray and meditate this stuff away. If we could, we all would. It's OK to not be OK, and it's OK to get help.

The above selection is taken from the following article:

Fitelson, Elizabeth; et al. Treatment of postpartum depression: clinical, psychological and pharmacological options. (Dec. 30, 2010). *International Journal of Women's Health*(3), 1-14. doi: 10.2147/IJWH.S6938.

Chapter 7:

Where NOT to go for help

It can be hard when you're starting out your treatment journey, especially if you don't have a built-in support network around you. While building a network online can seem like the easiest way to go about building your support network, do so with caution and with purpose. Some of the online venues out there can be seriously toxic and triggering to your treatment. Here are some things I've found that can be not so good for your mental health.

Mom groups

You ideally want to surround yourself with other moms. Who else can understand you like another mom? Surprisingly or not, in this age of the "do it all mommy," a lot of moms have a toxic view of motherhood and are less understanding of a mom who is visibly struggling with it. Be sure you're looking for a mom group that's openly discussing the hard topics and isn't just there to make you happy by getting your "mom bod" back. Look out for "playdates" where the kids just play and the moms are glued to their cell phones and not chatting. You've got to find a mom group where the moms are looking for support and are willing to share the good, the bad, and the ugly with other moms.

When my family and I moved 1,000 miles away from all our friends and family, I thought I'd found a mom group that would support me and my kids. But the second I got hit with PPD/anxiety for a second time and started to express my feelings and struggles, I was brushed off and dismissed. My walls came up, I left the group, and I fell into an even darker place than before. I don't recommend it.

<u>Facebook</u>

I don't think there's a more toxic place on the Internet than Facebook. The platform is just a dumpster fire of negativity. I only have it now for my business pages, and it's still hard not to get sucked into people's drama. If you're like me, and everything you read affects you, I recommend you stay off the platform or make sure you only follow people and groups that make you feel good about yourself. I found even postpartum depression support groups can be triggering, because everyone is having such a hard time, and reading someone else's struggle can make yours worse. It could help you channel your energy into helping them, but right now it's OK to be selfish and help yourself and your kids first. Then worry about everyone else.

Instagram

Personally, I love Instagram. There's a lot less room for negativity, but there's a lot more room for false imaging and false messaging. This is especially true if you follow any fitness accounts or mommy accounts where they make every meal look perfect, post creative photos with their kids, and show pictures of themselves in a bikini six months after giving birth. Good for them, but focusing on these types of accounts can bad for your mental health. If the accounts you follow make you feel bad, unfollow them.

Instagram is where I built my support network. I started sharing my experiences by posting illustrations and comics depicting my struggles. I found moms who were going through the same thing and whom I could really relate to. Some of these moms have become real friends whom I speak with on a regular basis. There's a lot to be said for the power of social media, but you have to be selective in how you use it, and you have to protect yourself.

The news

The world is a scary place these days; it probably always has been. Watching the news can be incredibly triggering. There's so much crime, so much political hubbub, and so many wars going on around the world. When your mental health is already fragile, paying too close attention to what's going on around the world can be too much to handle and weigh hard on your heart, so tread carefully. Maybe just read a newsletter a couple times a week or turn on NPR for the headlines, but take it easy until you're feeling back to normal.

Parenting magazines

I think parenting magazines mean well, but man, they sure do push the "do it all mommy" image. They're full of meal tips, playdate tips, activities you "should" be doing with your kids, and all of the products every parent "can't live without." It's overwhelming, and it can be really anxiety-inducing to pick up one of those magazine when you're already doubting everything you're doing. So don't. If you want to read a magazine, pick up Highlights for the kids or Psychology Today.

Random moms on the playground

When you're desperate for friends and people to understand, it can be tempting to open up to anyone within hearing range. My advice is to just go slowly. This is advice I could have benefited from hearing before I just went whole hog on some moms during my daughter's first year. It's like dating: you want to open up, but not too quickly, because you don't want to scare anyone away. All moms are dealing with a lot, so the last thing they want is another person to take care of. Try to slowly build that friendship and divulge bits and pieces of what you're dealing with, instead of unloading all at once. The good ones will stick around, listen, and give you their number to continue the convo and have playdates. But the bad ones will just smile, nod, and offer some excuse as to why they have to go and brush off your attempt to exchange numbers.

Making mom friends is so hard, but don't be discouraged. Remember it's more important to have one really good mom friend than five you can't speak your truth with.

The library (apparently!)

While writing this book, I went to the library with the intent of writing without distraction and doing some additional research for resources. But what I found was shocking and heartbreaking, and it illustrates how much work we need to do on spreading awareness and information on postpartum mood disorders.

I hope your library is better equipped than mine, but here was my experience.

I typed "postpartum depression," and then just "postpartum" into the library catalogue, hoping they'd generate different results. They didn't.

Here's a rundown of what I found. First of all, there were only 13 titles "that matched your search." THIRTEEN. One in seven women is diagnosed with a postpartum mood disorder, and yet only 13 books matched my search.

Scrolling through the list, the results got worse. The first book in the search was one about treating your thyroid to get your mental health back on track. I'm not saying this is wrong, but this is not what a mom who is desperate for some relief and understanding is looking for. Next was a fiction book by Patricia McDonald titled, From Cradle to Grave. Without having read it, I assume one of the characters in the book has postpartum depression. Entertaining? Sure. Helpful?

Probably not.

The only book in the list of 13 that could maybe be of any use on the subject was Brooke Shields' memoir, Down Came the Rain. I haven't read it, and nearly four years out from the birth of my first child, I don't think I could read it without being triggered.

The library is supposed to be a resource to and for the people, especially those who are low-income. Libraries can largely affect the minority population, who already have a hard time getting access to all types of care and to things like the internet, which many of us take for granted. Almost every community in the United States has a library, so every library should have resources for people with this kind of need, especially a need that's so common.

We'll address how we can get some of this changed in chapter 12. For now, if you're looking for additional resources outside of this book, use Google to search for some medical journal articles and books. Postpartum.net has some additional reading materials, as well.

Chapter 8:

You are not alone: Interviews with women who all walked a similar path and came out on the other side, battered but still standing

Dava Warner, military wife and mom of one

When did you realize there was something wrong?

I began to realize something was wrong when I started feeling "touched out" more frequently. Like I constantly had this new thing clinging to me 24/7, and I was nothing more than boobs (to put it frankly). It was then that I realized my baby has to be able to sense that feeling, and that's not okay. I wanted to distance myself from my brand new baby that I love endlessly. And that wasn't okay either. I would spontaneously cry when nursing, and I was stressed when she wasn't gaining weight right away. I felt that I wasn't doing enough, or worse: that if she had a different mom, they would do better and she would be doing better.

What led to you finally getting diagnosed and treated?

My husband. He told me one night, "Mental health is not a you or I thing. It's an us thing." That hit me hard. My postpartum mind made me feel alone, and he brought me back with just that one sentence. I knew that it was important to my family for me to not necessarily be happy, but to be healthy. That week, I made an appointment at out physician's office. I knew I was going back to work soon, and my job would no longer be protected if I took extra time to get my head back in the game. I wouldn't have any sick days for at least 30 days after I started back to take a "mental health day" (or 15) if I needed to. (Side note, I work for a mental health agency, for that extra piece of irony.)

What roadblocks did you face in your treatment?

I don't know if it's different in the civilian world, but seeing military doctors, it was frustrating. I felt like I wasn't being heard and was being brushed off, as this was "normal for new moms." They asked how much sleep I was getting, how much I was eating, and the standard, "Do you feel like hurting yourself or others?" And that was it for a while. It didn't help that the majority of them were men.

How did your diagnosis and struggle affect your family and your relationships?

It was stressful at times, because we didn't tell anyone about it. My husband and our doctors obviously knew, but we decided not to tell anyone else because we are states away from family and didn't want them to unnecessarily worry from afar. We were handling it and maintaining a close eye on everything, ready to let them know if it got to the point that we needed reinforcements. Sometimes it still feels like I was keeping a secret from them, almost like I was ashamed of it and that my own family would think that I was weak or not a good mom because of it, which I know is not the case.

What could your spouse or family have done to be more supportive during this time?

Considering my husband was the only one who knew, he was phenomenal. He was always ready and willing to do whatever it was I thought I needed. He reminded me to eat, sleep, and shower. He encouraged me to venture out of the house by myself if I was ready to. He was as supportive as he possibly could be.

What would have made it easier to cope with this diagnosis?

I FINALLY got a doctor that was listening to ME; not my medical chart or previous doctor's notes, but me. And this doctor was consistent. They wanted to be the only one to see me from then on out, which was great for me.

Did you have help outside of a therapist or psychiatrist (such as a mom group or family)?

I joined a MOMS Club chapter that really made a difference. Having support from other mommas who have been through it made me feel like I wasn't defective as a mom. I realized that although it's unfortunately "normal" for a lot of mommas, it was good that it was common, because then it wasn't taboo to talk about there. Moms would drop everything to help you out. Playdates, Moms' Nights Out, babysitting, porch drop offs when you or your little(s) were sick, secret mom gift swaps, educational speakers at meetings; it made all the difference.

What finally worked for you?

A culmination of things helped: acceptance, honest communication with my husband, pushing myself to take "me time" even if I still felt guilty about it, a mix of medication and homeopathic remedies, and finding a creative outlet for myself.

When did you finally start to feel a little more like yourself and able to bond with your child and spouse again?

Soon after being properly medicated. Having an autoimmune and hormonal disease, it was difficult figuring out what was PPD/PPA and what was a thyroid issue. When I could just play with my baby without any other thought in the world, I knew I was okay – or at least on the right path to get there.

What do you wish you'd known about Postpartum mood disorders before you were faced with one?

That it was okay. That it didn't make me any less of a mother. That my baby wouldn't hate me for needing a little bit of space. That it would come and go sometimes.

This may seem a bit redundant, but what was your experience with getting a diagnosis from your OB/GYN, midwife, and other doctors? Were they responsive or dismissive?

Originally, I only saw my OB/GYN or midwife for my two-week and six-week checkups. Then I was switched over to a family health physician. I remember taking our baby for one of her wellness visits. When the pediatrician casually asked how I was doing, I ended up bursting into tears saying, "Oh, I'm fine..." and it didn't faze them. They went on with her wellness visit, didn't ask anything else of me, and sent us home. Looking back on it, it still frustrates me.

What are some things you still struggle with? Do the anxieties and issues you faced in the beginning still creep up on you sometimes?

Sometimes now with our daughter sleeping through the night consistently, I'll wake up in a panic that something is going to happen to her and I won't know, because I'm used to her sleeping all night. So I sneak into her room to check that she's breathing. It doesn't happen nearly as often, but when it does, there is this sense of dire urgency that I can't explain.

What do you think are some of the biggest misconceptions PPD sufferers face?

That it's just the hormones. That we're just sad. That

we just don't want to be moms. That we just need to get over it. That it's just called parenthood. That PPD is something we can and should control. That PPD isn't a big deal because it's increasingly common. That PPD/PPA symptoms look the same cookie cutter way for every single sufferer.

Anything else?

I think it's so important as a new mom to casually check in on friends that are also new moms. It's important to offer no-strings-attached support, even if they are just an acquaintance or someone you kinda knew in school. You never know; you could be the only one offering them support during that time. You may be the only one in their life that may understand what they are feeling.

And another side note: I think it is absolutely ridiculous that some women in the U.S. may not get proper treatment due to mental illness services not being covered by their insurance, and they fear outrageous medical bills just to be seen by a doctor. It's worse for women who are without insurance at all. And God forbid that a woman in that situation has any suicidal thoughts or ideations.

Mala Barnard, mom of one

When did you realize something was wrong?

> When my baby was asleep and I looked out from the
> window and thought about hanging myself from a tree. I
> cried so hard and realized something was wrong with me.
> What finally led to you getting diagnosed and treated?
>
> I've been diagnosed since my six-week postpartum
> check-up, but I refused to take meds. I was so ignorant
> and hardheaded. I started the treatment after I had a
> miscarriage, right before my baby's second birthday. I
> always think my miscarriage was one of the universe's
> ways to push me to get help.

What roadblocks did you face in getting treatment?

Money. I don't have insurance. I'm not a U.S. citizen, yet. Treatment is expensive.

How did your diagnosis and struggle affect your family and your relationships?

I would say the first two years postpartum were the hardest. My husband didn't know, but I always thought I was going to lose him because in my mind, he hated me. But the more I learned about it, the more he did, too. It's getting better, but I wish more couples would talk about this so they can prepare themselves.

What could your spouse or family have done to be more supportive during this time?

Educate themselves. Help without being asked. Be patient, shut up, and listen. If you don't understand, shut up and listen. Also, understand that sometimes you can't fix a problem, but you can always be present.

What would have made it easier for you to cope with this diagnosis?

I don't know; maybe knowing I'm not alone. That I'm not

broken. That I'm not weak. I love how more and more people talk about this. It helps a lot.

Did you have help outside of a therapist or psychiatrist (such as a mom group or family)?

Instagram has been my family for the longest time. My family and friends are a million miles away. I did go to therapy for a while, but we kept moving. I got tired trying to new therapists.

What finally worked for you?

Medication, working out, not having high expectations, and letting my kid watch the iPad.

When did you finally start to feel a little more like yourself and able to bond with your child and spouse again?

After my son's 2nd birthday, I think. It's way better now. I also weaned myself from my meds and am trying to eat healthier and work out and say no unapologetically.

What do you wish you'd known about postpartum mood disorders before you were faced with one?

*I wish I'd known it was "normal" for moms to have this. I
wish I'd known it was okay to ask for help. I wish I'd known
I don't have to be strong all the time. I wish I'd known
parenting is not just for mom.*

**What was your experience with getting a diagnosis from
your OB/GYN, midwife, and other doctors? Were they
responsive or dismissive?**

*They offered me meds right away, but they said I couldn't
breastfeed. I learned later that I could still breastfeed, so
I wish they knew more about that. I also had a nurse that
came to my house every two weeks to check on me. So
that helped a lot.*

**Did you have to try several therapists or counselors before
you found the right one to really help you?**

Yes, definitely.

**What are some things you still struggle with? Do the
anxieties and issues you faced in the beginning still creep up
on you sometimes?**

Yes, I still have anxiety for family occasions, phone calls, and while I drive. I still always think of the worst that can happen

What do you think are some of the biggest misconceptions PPD sufferers face?

People always say, "Be grateful." People assume we are not grateful. We fucking are. Motherhood combined with PPD isn't easy.

Brittany Vanover, badass entrepreneur, wife, and mom of two

When did you realize there was something wrong?

After my son was born, he ended up in the NICU. I had a home birth, and like many babies, he needed a little help to get his breathing to where it should be right after being born. When my midwife realized that he needed the help right after birth, she had my doula call for an ambulance as a safety measure, in case it turned out to be serious and not just the need for a bit of help.

After a couple minutes he was completely fine, but it was decided we should go for a checkup at the hospital just to be safe. While there, we were treated horribly about having had a home birth ,and they said they had to admit him because, "We don't know what you exposed *him to, and he needs antibiotics." By that night, they told us he was having seizures and all sorts of problems, and they said he would have issues for probably his entire life. They had him medicated and hooked up to everything, just telling us terrible things and treating us poorly for my birth choice. It was an awful and traumatic experience.*

I lived in the hospital for an entire week, dealing with all the physical realities of just having had a baby, sleeping on a couch, and being told bad thing after bad thing. We eventually left the hospital, and it wasn't until a month later - when we scheduled his follow up appointment at a different hospital and went in for tests - that we were told the tests showed nothing and the new doctor couldn't find any sign of seizures or anything else. She took him off his medications. It left us feeling like the original hospital had been so bent on looking for a problem that they diagnosed him with things that weren't really true.

I felt paranoid about our original hospital stay, angry that my birth and postpartum had gone so off track, and sad. It was a lot to deal with, and I wasn't able to deal with it in a healthy way. As time went on, I just became more and more angry and anxious about everything. An accidental pregnancy six months later left me even more angry – which of course also made me feel guilty. I was mad about being pregnant when I was struggling so much and had yet to feel better mentally or emotionally, and I had to deal with the guilt of being mad about a baby whom of course I would love.

What led up to you finally getting diagnosed and treated? And if you didn't get help, why not? How did you get through it otherwise?

I resisted getting treatment for a few reasons. I was very adamant that I did not want to be medicated. I'm not super woo-woo, but I have always been one to medicate only as a last resort. I had home births and declined any pain medication, didn't take pain killers after a surgery because I didn't want the side effects, and I don't take anything stronger than Excedrin when I have a really bad headache. I didn't want to be told I now had to take medication every single day of my life in order to function. I decided I would power through, which backfired, of course. Two and a half years in, and after back-to-back pregnancies, I'm finally just coming to terms with the fact that I have to do it. Even though logically I know there is nothing to be embarrassed about, to admit that I need help of any kind is hard for me.

What roadblocks have you faced in getting treatment?

My biggest roadblock – now that I'm finally admitting I need help – is figuring out how to get it. I am not a doctor person; I don't think I've been to the doctor in ten years. I saw a midwife for my pregnancies, and the last time I remember going to a doctor (other than an OB/GYN for a pap smear or the dermatologist) was at least ten years ago. I'm overwhelmed. Do I see a therapist? A psychiatrist? A primary care physician? Being overwhelmed in figuring out what to do is yet another roadblock in a long journey to getting help.

How has your struggle affected your family and relationships?

It destroyed my marriage and made me incredibly difficult to be around. After two and a half years, the only reason I am finally ready to seek professional help is having been given an ultimatum: take the steps to fix this, or soon there won't be anything to fix. It was a wakeup call as to how my silent suffering was not so silent after all. My PPD has manifested as anger, mood swings, severe anxiety, and an inability to admit to or talk about any of it. It's made me irrational, difficult, and impossible to live with or be around.

What could your spouse or family have done to be more supportive during this time?

> I don't fault my husband for how he responded to my mental and emotional change. It was as new to him as it was to me, and neither of us had any experience in what was happening. Just as much as it affected me, it affected my family. Since I didn't seek help, he just got more and more frustrated and angry at how I was acting. He didn't know what to do, so he lashed out just as much as I did. It's been hard for him to be supportive, because in his eyes, it's as easy as just going to a doctor and getting 'fixed.' If I haven't done that, then I must not really be dealing with what I say I'm dealing with. He can't understand why someone would not seek help and isn't able to see it how I see it. He can't fathom why it's hard for me to admit I need help and seek it out.

What would have made it easier for you to cope with this diagnosis?

> It would have made things so much easier if I knew anyone in my real life who had been through the same thing and who would have given me someone I knew and trusted to talk to. The lack of support from anyone who

had actually experienced it was definitely a factor in me not wanting to admit what was going on.

Did you have help outside of a therapist or psychiatrist (such as a mom group or family)?

No. None of my friends have experience with this. As a stay-at-home working mom, most days I don't see or talk to anyone outside of my husband and kids. It's very isolating, which I'm sure also plays a huge role in my ability to cope or "get better."

What do you wish you'd known about postpartum mood disorders before you were faced with one?

That I wasn't safe from being affected just because I'd never had full-blown depression before. It really can happen to anyone.

What was your experience with getting a diagnosis from your OB/GYN, midwife, and other doctors? Were they responsive or dismissive?

Since I didn't seek help from my midwife, she wasn't able to help me. I have no doubt she would have, but I didn't truthfully answer questions at any of my postpartum visits. I thought I could handle it, I thought it would go away with time, and I didn't want to be told I needed medication. You can't help someone who won't be truthful and who doesn't want help.

What do you think are some of the biggest misconceptions PPD sufferers face?

That you could have avoided it if you had made different choices. It's out of our control; it can happen to anyone regardless of circumstance.

Anything else?

Sharing these stories is so important. I know the stigma around mental health issues is slowly being lifted, and the more these stories and experiences are told, the more people will feel comfortable getting help before their lives are even more affected by what's happening.

Ilana

When did you realize there was something wrong?

>When I looked at my one-month-old son and thought
about giving him up. For some reason, I couldn't bring
myself to feel anything when I saw him; like he wasn't real.

*What led up to you finally getting diagnosed and treated?
And if you didn't get help, why not? How did you get through
it otherwise?*

>I was open with my husband about my feelings. At first,
I was so ashamed I almost didn't come forward. Once I
spoke those words out loud, it was so freeing. I went to a
mommy group that had meetings about PPD, and just
talking it out helped.

What roadblocks did you face in getting treatment?

Shame. I thought that if you didn't immediately love your baby, there was something wrong with you. My PTSD did not help

How did your diagnosis and struggle affect your family and your relationships?

It caused my husband to pull away from me a bit, so our relationship was strained. After a while, we started being honest about our feelings and worries, and it truly helped.

What could your spouse or family have done to be more supportive during this time?

Read up on what I was going through.

What would have made it easier for you to cope with this diagnosis?

Some alone time. We were living paycheck to paycheck with me on leave. My husband worked double shifts to keep us afloat, leaving me alone with a baby and super stressed.

Did you have help outside of a therapist or psychiatrist (such as a mom group or family)?

A mommy group.

What finally worked for you?

Just talking it out with my husband, meditation, and getting some alone time to sit with my feelings.

When did you finally start to feel a little more like yourself and able to bond with your child and spouse again?

When my son turned one. I looked back and just realized I was going to be okay. The hard parts were done, and I had a support group and my husband behind me.

What do you wish you'd known about PPD and mood disorders before you were faced with one?

That it was normal and I wasn't losing my mind.

What was your experience with getting a diagnosis from your OB/GYN, midwife, and other doctors? Were they responsive or dismissive?

Very dismissive. She just brushed it off and told me to lose weight.

What are some things you still struggle with? Do the anxieties and issues you faced in the beginning still creep up on you sometimes?

I have other mental illnesses, so I never really recover. I've rekindled my love for art, and it has made my life so much better to have a creative outlet.

What do you think are some of the biggest misconceptions PPD sufferers face?

That we're just crying all the time. Most times, I was angry and I couldn't understand why.

Hannah

When did you realize there was something wrong?

> I couldn't relax, ever. I never wanted to hold my baby, but
> I didn't want to put her down. I was mourning the loss of
> my life before her and constantly anxious that she would
> wake up when she was sleeping. No matter how long she
> napped, it was never enough. I never had enough time
> without her.

What led up to you finally getting diagnosed and treated?
And if you didn't get help, why not? How did you get through
it otherwise?

> I cried every single day until my mom and husband told
> me it was time to go chat with my doctor. My mom came
> to the house and stayed for a week. She helped me cook

and clean, she held the baby so I could sleep, and she drove me to the doctor's office to get treatment. She also stood back, observed me with my baby, and assured me that I was a good mom.

What roadblocks did you face in getting treatment?

I didn't want to tell my doctor the truth. Luckily, he didn't ask much. He took my word for it and prescribed me medication.

How did your diagnosis and struggle affect your family and your relationships?

Everyone I told was so proud that I got help. It made me more willing to talk about how hard it is sometimes.

What could your spouse or family have done to be more supportive during this time?

Nothing. They were perfect.

Did you have help outside of a therapist or psychiatrist (such as a mom group or family)?

> My mom and my husband were there for me every day. My husband worked nights for a few weeks after my mom left so that I had some help during the day. Nobody pressured me to let relatives come over when it was too much for my anxious brain to handle. People were ready to help.

What finally worked for you?

> The support of my family, the medication, and taking a few shifts at work (probably before I physically should have) so that I could leave the house, It also helpd to understand that babies cry, and sometimes you have to just put them down somewhere safe and let them cry for a minute, so you can go take a shower for your own benefit.

When did you finally start to feel a little more like yourself and able to bond with your child and spouse again?

> With my husband, it was when he promised me over and over again that he wanted this baby as much as I did, and that he loved her and didn't regret having her like I

did. It also helped when we got to go and get a beer for an hour while my mom watched her. With my daughter, I think it was when I started to get a routine. I was almost robotic at first. It was the same thing every morning: I'd get up, make coffee, shower, put three types of lotion on different parts of my body, get dressed, braid my hair, sit outside with my coffee, and wait until she woke up. In my routine, I found peace to calm my anxious and sad mind, and I was able to love her.

What do you wish you'd known about PPD and mood disorders before you were faced with one?

That it's really scary, but having a newborn doesn't last forever. If you have a history of mood disorders, you'll probably develop one postpartum.

What was your experience with getting a diagnosis from your OB/GYN, midwife, and other doctors? Were they responsive or dismissive?

I am happy my doctor was so willing to go with what I felt. But I wish he'd pushed a bit harder for me to tell the full truth of how bad I really felt.

Did you have to try several therapists or counselors before you found the right one to really help you?

No.

What are some things you still struggle with? Do the anxieties and issues you faced in the beginning still creep up on you sometimes?

I feel that I missed out on enjoying my daughter when she was tiny. I feel guilty for feeling so much coldness toward her. I wish I could've been a better mama when she was new to the world and just as scared and uncomfortable as I was.

What do you think are some of the biggest misconceptions PPD sufferers face?

It's not just the blues. It's really fucking scary and debilitating. We need help. Sometimes women hurt their babies, and sometimes they don't, but we should be able to talk freely about our feelings without feeling like we will get our children taken away.

Is there anything else you feel like sharing that I didn't ask?

I didn't hurt her, I didn't neglect her, and I didn't mistreat her. But for those first few weeks, I didn't want her to wake up when she slept. I wanted something to happen to her, and I wanted her to go away. I regretted ever getting pregnant. I thought I ruined my life. I thought I trapped my husband and ruined his life – although our pregnancy was 100 percent planned, and both of us were totally ready to have a **baby. I cried every day and** compulsively Googled when this would go away, if it ever got better, and if I was a bad mom. But when it got better, I fell in love. I'm a great mom, and she's the most amazing little person. I wish I could've been there 100 percent right from the beginning, but I work hard to be completely present for her now.

And now for something a little different.

This next woman is a nurse, mother, and now a grandmother. Her experience is that of a daughter whose mother struggled with depression, a new mother who suffered from postpartum depression, a nurse who saw patients struggle to deal with the disease, and a mother who watched her own daughter struggle.

Because she is sharing her family's experience, we are keeping her anonymous.

When did you realize there was something wrong?

I was 25 years old in 1983. I delivered my second baby vaginally with no drugs at all. It wasn't a problem pregnancy or a traumatic birth. I had no health issues. I was happily married and had no financial issues. I was a stay-at-home mom.

I wasn't treated like I was a tired or hysterical woman. I think my family (husband, parents, and in-laws) knew that something was more wrong than that. I was so out of character. My very first symptom was not one to be very concerned about in the beginning: I couldn't sleep or fall asleep. If I slept, it was in very short intervals with intrusive thoughts. I knew something wasn't right. I also was a second-time-mom in under two years, so my infant daughter went directly in her crib from the first night home. Her bedroom was directly across from ours, and we kept the doors open. Also, this newborn was so calm and not as needy as my first. She slept well, drank her bottles, and had no problem with her bowel movements. She was so different from my first, who screamed day and night.

This second baby was a dream, and then at exactly one week old, I couldn't sleep one night. It was as if I was on stimulants. I tried all the things you would think might affect sleep; cutting out caffeine and chocolate. I tried sleep teas and foot massages. But as the days went by, I became so sleep-deprived that even my circadian rhythm was out of whack. I lost my appetite and couldn't eat. I remember trying to force foods that would go down my throat easily because I knew I needed nutrition. I remember opening a can of chicken noodle soup and gagging as I tried to eat it. One day, my parents came over to give me a break and told me to get in my car and just go somewhere. It was early evening, and in those days I ate Arby's roast beef (I'm now 99 percent plant based and haven't had red meat, pork, or veal in over 25 years). I went into Arby's and ordered my roast beef sandwich with their special sauce. I just sat there and worried that I would never have an appetite again as I tried to force this sandwich down. I looked around at all the "normal" people sitting, eating, and chatting, and that's when I knew I needed help. I had no desire to eat or socialize.

I phoned my OB/GYN to explain my situation. He was very understanding and ordered a prescription for Vistaril. He said it would help me sleep and told me not to worry, because I'd still hear my baby during the night for feedings. I took the pill the first night, and it worked. I thought it was a miracle. I thought my problems were solved. I continued to take it before bed, but within one week, it slowly stopped working and I started to panic. Now bedtime was a nightmare, and daytime was just as bad. One night I laid wide awake and could feel my body vibrating in the bed. I was so restless trying to settle my mind, but my brain wouldn't allow it. I thought I was losing my mind. And this wasn't a figure of speech. I jumped out of bed and threw my body against the blank wall to prove to myself that I could feel the cold wall against my skin. It sounds dramatic, but I was desperate. It felt like a train was going through our yard and my body was rattling from the train's vibration. I knew I was in trouble, because there were no trains in our neighborhood. My parents' house was across the street from train tracks, so I knew how it felt to be sleeping when a train went by.

I called my OB/GYN in the morning and told him the pills stopped working. I needed sleep to function and to take care of an infant and my daughter, who wasn't even two years old yet. He listened and very calmly told me I needed to make an appointment with a psychiatrist. My world shattered when I heard those words. I started crying. He told me I had gone beyond baby blues. I had lost all my baby weight and close to 40 pounds in a few weeks. At that time, my maternal first cousin had similar symptoms and found a psychiatrist who was treating her. She was admitted to the local psychiatric hospital and put on meds. I was still pregnant at the time and went to visit her. She recommended her psychiatrist. I called that day and made an appointment with her doctor. I had no idea what he would tell me or how he could help but I had to hang on to every shred of hope for help.

The appointment was over a week away, and I started slipping deeper and deeper into a depression with horrible anxiety. I went to the appointment. My husband waited in the waiting room while I saw the doctor. The doctor had two other doctors in the room (they may have been students, interns, or residents, I don't remember). He knew my cousin was being treated for postpartum depression, so he had some history. He didn't mention her, but he knew we were related. The doctor asked me several questions. One of the questions he asked was about what led me to come to his office. My brain – not functioning properly – answered that my husband drove me and that he was downstairs in the waiting room. That was not how I was supposed to answer. I was supposed to tell him the sequence of events that led me to him that day. I just remember being confused and thinking some of the questions were dumb, such as whether I had thoughts about harming myself or my baby. My answer was, truthfully, "No." He told me his recommendation was that I be admitted to the local psychiatric hospital immediately without going home to pack. My husband was called into the room.

The doctor explained my illness. We then left the doctor's office and went directly to the hospital. My parents babysat my children. My husband brought my personal belongings to the hospital later. I stayed as an inpatient for ten days. I was put on sleeping meds, anti-anxiety meds, and Lithium. I was titrated up to a so-called "therapeutic level" and had blood drawn every day. My daughter was born February 17th. I must have entered the hospital around March 20th, because we celebrated my older daughter's birthday – March 26th – in the hospital. Of course, we didn't have candles and we used plastic utensils, celebrating in one of the larger visitor rooms that the staff reserved just for us. Lithium was supposed to be this wonder drug, and I was on it for several months, but it tore up my stomach. I went to a gastroenterologist and was told it was the Lithium causing my pain.

That's when I started switching different anti-depressants; starting a new one and waiting to see if it worked. Within two years I only became more depressed, and the anxiety turned into agoraphobia. I was a mess. I couldn't drive without a true panic attack, and I became housebound. I couldn't be home alone without a family member or friend until my husband got home from work. Needless to say, none of this was pleasant. Finally, in June 1985, my doctor recommended admission to the hospital for electro convulsive therapy (ECT), also known as "shock treatments."

I was 28 years old and a mess, but I was desperate again for help. I was off to the hospital again while my parents babysat my then two- and four-year-old daughters. This time, the hospital stay was for a month. I had an ECT treatment every other weekday. I was allowed a day pass or two. The day I was discharged, my mother-in-law was being treated for breast cancer as an inpatient at the general hospital. My husband picked me up, and we went directly to the general hospital to see his mother. When we arrived, she was in a coma. We kissed her and went home. When we got home, we received the call that she had passed. It was a very sad day.

How have your daughters fared?

I've always had concerns about whether my daughters would suffer from PPD if they got pregnant. My older daughter has two children, who are now one and three years old. She had mild-to-normal hormonal baby blues for a day or two. I was watching her like a hawk. Both my daughters know my history, so the concern was always there.

My younger daughter is 36 years old. She has a three-year-old and a four-month-old. She had a miscarriage *one year before having her second baby. I was always more concerned for her, because she had been treated off and on for depression and anxiety since she was 15 years old. Both my daughters made their OB/GYN doctors aware of my PPD history. The doctor offered to put my youngest daughter on a "safe" anti-depressant while pregnant, but she refused. She did take meds for a short time after her first pregnancy and after the miscarriage. She also started to take meds after her most recent pregnancy, when the baby was about two months old. I'm not surprised, but at least the meds work. I was also very concerned for her because she lives in Florida, and I live in Buffalo, New York. I made her husband aware of how serious PPD could be and what to look for, especially how it affects sleep. He is very supportive and patient with her.*

How have attitudes about treatment changed over time?

The doctors today know more and recognize PPD more than in the 1980s. At least I received good care from knowledgeable doctors, but my body didn't respond to the meds as readily as expected. I must say, the ECT treatments worked for me. After the month-long stay, I had to return for overnight hospital stays for what they called a "maintenance ECT treatment." These were once a month for about six months, then every other month for about six months, and then once every few months for about six or eight months; I don't remember exactly. I say the treatments saved my life. I will say they saved my mother's life, too. My brother was her third child - all natural and without a traumatic birth. She suffered for four years, both on and off medications as an outpatient. They called it a nervous breakdown, at the time.

I'm four years older than my brother. I guess the doctors and my family blamed my mother's condition on her circumstances. My dad was a Korean War veteran who would now be diagnosed with Post Traumatic Stress Syndrome. He couldn't keep a job, and they were broke. They couldn't pay their bills, filed bankruptcy, and my dad started to drink. At the time, my mother's meds didn't work. I was seven years old, my brother was four, and my sister was ten. My mom was admitted to the state psychiatric hospital for months. She received ECT treatments, as well. I remember my dad telling me that she would be home in time for my First Holy Communion, and she was. She returned home and was the strongest woman in our family. Everyone came to her for advice and with their personal and family problems. She was the voice of reason and wisdom. You'd never know about her personal struggles with PPD if you had only just met her.

Over the years, her new friends and coworkers never knew her history. It is the same with me; only my family and very close friends are aware of my history. I didn't share my history with coworkers, neighbors, or new friends. There is a stigma attached to mental illness that I hope will be erased someday. Hopefully, PPD will be more readily diagnosed and treated.

How did you become a nurse?

I graduated from nursing school in 1995. It was the hardest thing I ever did, but I did it. It was a big accomplishment to become a registered professional nurse with two kids, a husband, a house, and a dog. In my last semester, my dad was diagnosed with terminal lung cancer. I went to my nursing advisor and explained that I needed to take a leave of absence to help my parents. My mom never had a driver's license, my sister lived in the suburbs, my brother worked full time and had a new baby on the way, and I would be the one to take my dad for his cancer treatments.

My advisor said, "No way. You continue on, and if I think your grades or skills are slipping, I'll let you know." It was the best advice. I studied and brought my books to all his appointments. He got to see me graduate in June and pass my boards the first time. He passed away that October, 1995. Nursing school was a godsend, because I ended up getting a divorce in 1998. It's a long story, but that's also when my daughter started to have her mental health problems. I'm sure it's all related. My children's father abandoned us. We had to move in with my mother, as we lost our house to foreclosure. Three weeks after we moved in with her, she was diagnosed with pancreatic cander and died less than a year later.

Thank God I had my nursing license and the help of family. It was a tough time for my girls. My doctor wanted to put me on medication prophylactically because of my situation, but I didn't think I needed any. I am a survivor; a strong and confident woman with two strong and confident daughters. My story may not be like the common experience today, because the meds are so much more reliable now, thank God. I see the meds working for my daughter. I read as much as I can about PPD, and I hope doctors are using the diagnosing tools to nip PPD in the bud. Even pediatricians are given a checklist to look for PPD in new moms.

Maybe if the meds had been more therapeutic for me

in the 1980s, I wouldn't have had to suffer - but then I wouldn't be who I am today. Suffering builds character. I also strongly believe in the power of prayer, and let me tell you, I prayed so hard during those times.

How are you now?

I have been very happily married for almost 13 years, to the most wonderful man. He is my rock. We are soul mates. He knows all about my mental health history. He knows about my daughter, too, and he supports her like a father.

I had no issues with medical bills because at the time, we had great health insurance coverage and we were able to afford any copays or unpaid balances.

I had no nursing training on PPD or mood disorders. I did, however, apply to work as an RN at the same psychiatric hospital in which I was treated. I was inspired to help mothers like myself. I thought I could help because I had the personal experience. I was hired per diem. It was my first nursing job. But by the time I was hired, most of the patients on the floors were elderly, depressed, or in drug rehab. I mostly worked on the adolescent unit, which was *an experience in itself. I left that hospital to work in a pediatrician's office, and then I worked as a school nurse for over 20 years. I've always thought about sharing my story but didn't know if it would really make a difference or help someone.*

Chapter 9:

For and about dads and partners

Dads can be depressed, too.

This may come as a shock, but men can also suffer from postpartum depression. Studies seem to vary, but the most common number I've found is ten percent of fathers who live with their children and experience depressive symptoms during the first five years of their child's life. I don't know how many fathers live with their kids, but ten percent is still a pretty big number. And I bet with a number that high, there are instances where both parents are dealing with the same thing. I can't begin to imagine how hard that would be.

Whether you're reading this as a wife or partner of a husband who's showing symptoms, or as a husband who is looking for answers for himself or his partner, **here's what some of the signs and symptoms can look like in men:**

- *Frustration or irritability*

- *Getting stressed easily*

- *Feeling discouraged*

- *Increasing complaints about physical problems such as headaches, digestion problems, or pain*

- *Problems with concentration*

- *Fatigue*

- *Lack of motivation*

- *Loss of interest in work, hobbies, and sex*

- *Isolation from family and friends*

- *Working constantly*

- *Increased anger and conflict with others*

- *Increased use of alcohol or other drugs*

- *Misuse of prescription medication*

- *Violent behavior*

- *Impulsiveness and taking risks like reckless driving and extramarital sex*

- *Thoughts of suicide*

If your partner is showing any of these symptoms, talk with them gently about what's going on. Refer them to the crisis text line if it's an emergency, or use the following resources:

- **Postpartum Support International's Dads Chat with an Expert**

    - A free facilitated phone call with one of our experts in pregnancy and postpartum mental health and family support

    - First Monday of every month. 8 p.m. Eastern, 5 p.m. Pacific, 7 p.m. Central. Call-in number: 1-800-944-8766, use code 73162#.

- **www.postpartumdad.org for more resources for postpartum fathers.**

    - They've also got a Facebook group you can join. Learn more about it via the website. Email the coordinator at info@postpartumdads.org.

WORLD'S
BEST
DAD

How to help moms

Dads, if you're reading this, you're likely your wife's or partner's main support system. You're her lifeline, her rock, and also her giant pain in the ass. In the throes of postpartum depression and anxiety, I didn't always appreciate my husband and all he was doing to help keep me alive, healthy, and happy. I still don't, but I'm working on it. If you've borne the brunt of your partner's anger, frustration, tears, and desperation, please don't take it personally. Unless you're being abusive, please know that no matter what we say, we love you and we're glad you're with us, but we're scared, we're tired, we're desperate, and we just want our pain to stop.

But how can you help? My husband still wonders about this. Here are some general tips. I promise, just knowing you're trying is a massive step in the right direction.

- **Reassure her** this is not her fault; she is not alone and she will get better. But it might not be quick, and it won't be easy, so please don't make light of it. Don't say, "You'll get past it," - as if it's a test we've got to take. You've got to make it sound like it's a grueling marathon, but we're going to cross the finish line together. Mental health is a long road, especially when you're trying to keep tiny humans alive. So never minimize her feelings, but let her know you're going to be there for all of it and that together, you will get her through this.

- **Encourage her** to talk about her feelings, and listen without judgment. Don't offer suggestions on what she should do; we don't want that unless we ask for it directly. Just listen. And sometimes, say, "That super sucks. I'm really sorry you're having to deal with this," or, "I know this seems so unfair, but you're doing a really amazing job." And then say lots of "I love you." You've got to talk to her like an adult so that she can feel like a human being again. The newborn phase, the teething stages; it all makes us feel like disgusting, milk-soiled, larger-than-our-normal selves, icky blobs. Those of us who stay home don't get to speak to another adult without baby babble all day until you get home. So make us feel like adults. Talk to us about stuff and ask us to talk about stuff. We know you've had a hard day too, but you have no idea how much we need you right now.

- **Help** with housework before she asks you. I cannot stress this one enough! There's nothing a struggling mom wants to less more than, "What do you need help with?" or, "What do you want for dinner?" We don't know! Rather than figuring out what we want, we get frustrated and think it'll be easier to just do it all ourselves. Because what we actually want right now is sleep, a shower, our boobs to stop hurting, and our nipples to stop bleeding. We want to stop feeling so angry and crying all the time. We want to stop being so scared to be alone with our kids. So instead, please say, "I did the laundry, the bottles are clean, and the sheets have been changed. Do you want a snack or coffee before I go hang out with our kid?" That is music to our ears. When you ask us what we want or need, it feels like a chore - like you're doing something because we're incapable of it. We already feel so incapable of everything else. I'm sorry, because I know it's a lot of work. But you've got to be our champion, our rock, and our protector; someone who's going to stand up to the dishes and the demons to help us through this.

- **Encourage her to take time for herself.** Breaks are a necessity; fatigue is a major contributing factor to worsening symptoms. I know this is a struggle for a lot of new moms, especially if they are breastfeeding. Suggest that she pump while your baby naps so that on the weekend, you can take over feedings and she can go to a movie, hang out with friends, get her nails done, or simply sleep for a few uninterrupted hours. It's going to be hard for her to give up that control, but it's an argument worth having, and she'll feel better after.

- **Don't expect her to be Super Housewife just because she's home all day.** Fuck yes to this. We have a job, too: keeping the baby (or babies) alive, fed, and entertained. It's a 24-hour job. We don't get a lunch break, we don't get to pee in peace, and we don't get to talk to adults. We are working all the time and on very little sleep. While driving 30 minutes to your job is not a vacation, it is a break. It's a timeout from the chaos, and it's one we don't currently get.

- **Be realistic** about what time you'll be home, and come home on time. Stick to a routine. My husband and I made family dinners a must when we moved to Texas. Every night, though sometimes he might be a little late, we all sit down at a table together and eat.

When I was breastfeeding, I breastfed my daughter at the table so we could still all eat together. Consistency and routine are incredibly important, because life with kids is just pure chaos.

- **Help her reach out to others for support and treatment.** This may be tricky, especially if she's in denial. Find out what your health insurance covers in terms of care, such as psychiatrists, counselors, and medication. Look for a group of providers in your area that are covered. You can also pull up the Postpartum Support International's local coordinators for your area. Or you can do what my husband did, though it did result in an argument. He told my friends. He had their numbers, and he told them what was happening and asked if they would come visit. He was scared, and he didn't know what else to do. I was pissed he did it; it wasn't his place. But months later, I understood why he did it, and I was grateful for a week with one of my best friends by my side. So it's worth the argument, in my opinion, especially if her friends are as amazing as mine.

- **Schedule some dates** with her and work together to find a babysitter. You can also do "family dates" if she's anxious about leaving the baby with anyone. There's a lot you can do with a kid in tow. If you have family in town that you trust, take advantage of it. Start with short dates such as lunch, dinner, or a movie; something close that you can leave if you need to.

- Offer simple affection and physical comfort, but **be patient if she is not up for sex.** It's normal for her to have a low sex drive with depression, and rest and recovery will help to bring it back. There's nothing worse than feeling stressed and miserable and then having your husband guilt you into sex. I know you're not guilting her into sex, but it feels like nagging, pressuring, and making her feel bad for not wanting to have anything to do with you. Again, we know that's not what you're actually doing, but that's what it feels like. Don't take it personally. We just don't want to be touched right now, and the idea of touching someone else - besides the baby who's been glued to us 24/7 - is just more work, and we're exhausted. Give us time.

Dealing with her anger and irritability

- Do what you can to make sure she eats regularly throughout the day, because low blood sugar results in a low mood and frustration. Have healthy and easy snacks on hand. Especially if she's breastfeeding, "hanger" is a real thing, and it's a doozy when it hits during all of this.

- Do your best to listen for the real request at the heart of her frustration. Reduce conflict by telling her, "I know we can work this out. I am listening."

- Keep the lines of communication open. Verbalize your feelings instead of distancing from her. It is helpful to take a break if your tempers are hot, but do get back to communicating. Don't just storm off. Take a deep breath if you can and say, "Look, I just need a minute. We can keep talking about this in ten minutes, and I just don't want this to turn into a huge fight."

- If she is expressing anger in such a way that you can't stay supportive, you might say something like, "I want to listen to you. I know this is important, but I'm having a hard time because you're so mad at me. Can we take a break and talk about it later?"

- Ask her how you can help right now. If she doesn't know how, make some suggestions. Again, tread lightly, speak softly, and don't make her feel like she's bad at everything. Just offer to take some things off her plate, such as bottles, washing onesies, emptying the diaper genie, and whatever else she may need.

I know this phase in your life, marriage, or partnership seems insane and insanely hard. But you can do it. This may be your biggest challenge yet as a couple, but if you can get through this, you get through anything - I'm sure of it. Keep trying and keep caring.

Chapter 10:

Creating your safe space

Finding an outlet when you're a new mom is so hard, and it's harder when you're dealing with postpartum depression. I know not all of these suggestions will work for everyone, but here are some of the things that helped me. Hopefully they can help you build a safe little space that you can use to unwind, unpack everything going around you, and help you feel more like yourself, even if just for a little bit - at least until your next therapy session.

Be creative

I've been doing crafts since I was a kid, so this was kind of a must for me. Once I had kids, though, we moved to our new house and a playroom took over everything. I no longer had room to paint and do mixed media paintings. Instead, I started using my phone and a stylus to doodle during breastfeeding sessions. This led to my getting an iPad for my next birthday, which resulted in me starting my business: MamaBear Creative.

Sometimes you just have to do something. Doodle on a napkin, keep a notebook by the breastfeeding area, keep crayons somewhere so you can doodle with the kids, or do whatever you can to tap into that side of your brain. And keeping it simple is imperative, because I know you don't have time, space, or energy right now.

When you find something you enjoy doing, share it with friends and family. Let them see what you're doing and start a conversation. If you don't have that kind of support near you, start an Instagram page. You'd be amazed at how many incredible makers and moms you'll meet on there who want to support you in your journey. You can also keep it completely personal and for your eyes only. There are no rules. Do what makes you feel good.

Read

Since moms get very little outside adult interaction - especially if you decide to stay at home - it's imperative you find ways to use your brain. When I breastfed my son - because he ate around the clock - I started devouring books on my phone using the Kindle app. I read the entire Sooki Stackhouse series and God knows how many other books. I've accidentally almost reread some books until I get a chapter or so in and then realize I read it two years ago in a breastfeeding haze. But it's important to keep your mind engaged, because it helps in those really dark nights when you're feeling like you can't possibly keep doing this. You can. You will. You just gotta find what works to help you keep on keepin' on.

Audio books work well, too. So invest in a pair of Bluetooth headphones and tune in. My kids loved listening to the Harry Potter audiobooks, so turn one of those on and enjoy some quiet time with the babe, if that's your cup of tea!

Listen to podcasts

If you don't already, do yourself a favor and download the podcasts My Favorite Murder, The Fall Line, Nothing Rhymes With Murder, Crime Junkie, Criminal, and Spooked ... oh and Sinisterhood. These podcasts have gotten me through some horrible times. Yes, they're all mostly about horrible crimes, but they're told by very funny, empathetic, and empowering women with a message of, "Shitty things happen, but you've got this."

If true crime isn't your thing, that's OK. There are a ton of other podcasts available out there. One that helped my friend who also suffered from PPD is the One Bad Mother podcast. I tried that one; it wasn't for me. I'm picky about voices. They also have One Bad Mother Facebook groups, where you can talk to moms from all over the world. This is a group that I found triggering, however, and I had to get off it. But my friend loves it. There's something for everyone out there, so find what works for you.

Get out of the house

If you find a mom you like somewhere, such as in line at Jamba Juice or Trader Joes, make a playdate, even if your kid seems too young for the playground or playdates. We all know it's intended more for you, and that's OK. Moms need playdates, too. It's hard to make yourself vulnerable (gosh do I know this), but like Brene Brown writes in Daring Greatly, when you make yourself vulnerable, you open yourself up to great things. (Also, if you haven't read her book yet, I highly recommend it.)

Be selfish

I'm sure you've heard the mantra, "Self-Care Isn't Selfish." That is absolutely true, now more than ever. But also, here's my mantra for moms: IT'S OK TO BE SELFISH! You are in a position right now that requires you to be selfish. You have to be selfish with your boundaries, and you have to be protective of yourself, your mental health, your kids, and your family. You've got to say no to the things that make you uncomfortable, that are triggering, and that cause you too much anxiety right now. These things won't always bother you, but for right now, you've got to create a bubble. You might make an exception for therapy and other necessary doctor appointments, and probably for grocery shopping (although Amazon Prime Now and grocery pick-up or delivery at your local grocery store are lifesavers for moms). Just trust your gut. On the days where you feel like you have more tolerance for things, branch out. On the days where you feel like making a decision - other than, "What's for breakfast?" - is too much to handle, don't push it. You have to be really protective of your mental health and your boundaries. Trust your gut and give yourself time to heal. You will get better.

Also, despite what parenting articles claim annually, screen time will not kill your kids. So if you need 20-40 minutes to get something done, shower, or sit without chasing your kids around the house, let them watch TV or use the iPad. They'll be fine.

Chapter 11:

Advocacy: How to build a safer and more supportive place for moms and women in the U.S.

Apparently the United States (I can't decide if I'm surprised or not) does not track suicide rates - especially those of postpartum women. I believe - from a reporter's point of view - that this is because suicide is still a very taboo subject here. A lot of families don't want it reported that their loved one died from suicide. It's hard knowing someone you loved took their own life. I get that. But for science, for information, it's important to let people know. There's no shame in letting people know that someone you loved struggled with what was happening to them. It's a struggle hundreds of thousands (maybe millions) of people face daily. We should be talking about it.

That said, suicide is the second leading cause of death for postpartum women. We know that much, but we don't really know the numbers here in the U.S. Based on studies done in Denmark and Canada, it seems about five percent of postpartum deaths are the result of suicide.

A 2019 study of more than one million women by two doctors in California found that maternal drug-related deaths and suicide were the second leading cause of postpartum death in that state. The study found that 74 percent of the women included in the study had made one or more visit to the emergency room to receive help and said this should have been where intervention occurred to further prevent their deaths.

An earlier 2005 study pointed out that while exact numbers aren't available for the whole of the U.S. postpartum population, suicides account for up to 20 percent of postpartum deaths. The study states, "Self-harm ideation is more common than attempts or deaths, with thoughts of self-harm during pregnancy and the postpartum ranging from five to 14 percent. The risk for suicidality is significantly elevated among depressed women during the perinatal period, and suicide has been found to be the second or leading cause of death in this depressed population."

I know this is all hard to hear, but I mention it because we need doctors, hospitals, families, and law enforcement to track this information so we can create a better screening, diagnosis, and treatment program for women suffering from postpartum mood disorders. These disorders are treatable, but we have to be proactive. We have to catch it early, we've got to follow-up with these women, and we've got to just keep up on it like we would any other chronic health disorder.

So how do we do this?

I hate it, but one of the main ways we can affect change is to lobby congress. If it's easier, start local. Start with your state legislators and get this issue in front of their faces. Once you feel heard, take it to your U.S. Senator and Representative, and make them listen. I don't care where you stand politically, it's been proven time and time again that women's health and women's issues matter little politically, even though we are no longer a minority. We are - physically - a majority in this country, and yet men still control our houses of government.

Where was I ... oh yes, lobby! Write your senators, congressmen, governors, and the White House. Start a change.org petition. Do whatever you need to do to draw attention to this case. Get this book and others like it in people's hands. Encourage your doctor, your therapist, your preacher, and your neighbor to be a champion for this cause. You don't have to share your story to make an impact, but it does help.

In 1999 the U.S. House did pass resolution 51, which proposed the National Institutes of Health further study postpartum illnesses and encouraged health care providers to "teach women about the prevalence, symptoms and treatment of postpartum depression." But here we are still with one in seven/five/nine (depending on the study) women being diagnosed with a postpartum mood disorder, and up to 20 percent of those women are dying by suicide. So there's a lot of work still to be done.

I believe the problem with access to care and treatment lies with insurance companies, because they don't actually seem to care about people. For them, it's all about money, and nothing will happen until we get congress to back this, because - sadly - money talks. And until insurance companies feel like their money isn't making an impact in Washington, will they actually start listening to what Washington is saying. That means we have to be louder than what they can spend on wining and dining our congressmen and congresswomen.

One of the organizations I found working to make changes in Washington is 2020 MOM (https://www.2020mom.org/).

I also found **The March for Moms Association**. So far,

they've had two successful marches on Washington to spread awareness about maternal health and everything it encompasses. This organization gives me hope because they've got a lot of great people involved with the march, which speaks to its authenticity and objectivity in making moms their priority.

Check them out at http://www.marchformoms.org.

When it comes to maternal health, you've got to know that maternal mortality is very high for women of color and low-income women in the United States. Even though we are in the top three richest countries in the world, we have more women dying in childbirth and up to one year post childbirth than many underdeveloped countries. A lot of this has to do with access to care and preexisting conditions that weren't treated during pregnancy or after with appropriate follow-up visits.

We need low-cost options in all communities. Whether it be through free clinics, the health department, or other options, women should be able to get comprehensive care, no matter their income level or racial makeup. Again, this goes all the way to the top; we've got to petition for affordable healthcare for all. That can be done on the town, city, state, and federal level, because women everywhere need access to care.

I am saying this a privileged white person who could afford care and still nearly bankrupted my family's savings.

We all (not just moms) need affordable and accessible mental healthcare, which is another issue to lobby for. This needs to be available to everyone everywhere, and insurance needs to cover it. And by covering it, I mean insurance companies need to pay these counselors, therapists, and psychiatrists what they're worth so that they're not having to charge their patients upwards of $100 per 35-45 minutes for care. We also need to make sure that women in low-income areas have access to mental healthcare. Studies have shown (as was written about in an issue of the Economist) that even having an untrained "counselor" to talk to can help people struggling with depression and anxiety. For more severe cases, a trained psychiatrist and therapist are warranted, but in other cases, something is better than nothing.

Knowledge is power

We've got to get more information about postpartum mental health into libraries, which are the main source of information for low-income and minority populations. How do we do this? Ask your librarians if they can get more books about postpartum health. If they say no, take it to the Friends of the Library, which helps fund your library. If they put up a fight, take it to the city or county council that funds the library. I doubt you'd need to do anything but ask the librarian. But let's say you live in some horrible place that just refuses to acknowledge the existence of postpartum mood disorders and women's health. In that case, you can take it to the American Library Association and get them to back you up on getting these resources into your library and community. You can learn more about them at http://www.ala.org.

Share your story

Talk to your doctors about getting more PPD resources into their office so that all patients know they exist. I believe all moms - not just those dealing with these disorders - need to know about them, because they need to know how to help their fellow mom. Empathy and kindness cost us nothing.

March

March on Washington, in your city, in your state capital; march to make yourself heard. Let them know you want insurance companies to cover these illnesses and to provide access to low-income families at prices they can pay or for free, because it'll save everyone money in the long run.

Go old school

Write to speakers and writers, and ask them to do a reading where you live. Bring up the topic at a mom's group, at the play gym, and wherever else you go. Get resources into the hands of the people who need them. There's no reason any of this should be hidden and limited to the people who are suffering. Knowledge is power, after all.

Go old school

Chapter 12:

Training for professionals and everyone else

I've mentioned it throughout this book (and you've likely experienced it yourself), but in general, healthcare professionals who are working with women are grossly undertrained and unprepared to deal with women's mental health issues - postpartum or not. In my OB/GYN's office, I never saw a pamphlet or magazine or anything else about postpartum mood disorder help or symptoms. There's nothing in there about mental health, period. This has to change. There should be postpartum resources in every general practitioner's office, every pediatrician's office, and especially in every OB/GYN's office. It should replace those freakin' BMI charts and other irrelevant checklists and pharmaceutical pamphlets that are all over the place. But that won't happen unless we ask for the information, demand it, and then refer them to the resources they need to get better informed.

As with much of the information in this book, the most comprehensive training and resource guides I've found come from Postpartum Support International (PSI). They hold annual conferences and have trainings throughout the year. They also have pamphlets and other materials physicians can request.

If you are a doctor, nurse, NP, therapist, social worker, or any other medical practitioner reading this, please request this information for your office, and be a part of doing more for women. No woman should fear telling her doctor what is going on mentally and emotionally postpartum, and women shouldn't fear Child Protective Services being called on them. This has actually happened to women in the U.S., and it absolutely should never happen.

You can request information at www.postpartum.net. Once there, you can see the upcoming conference info, sign up for a training, and request a number of materials. Your patients will thank you.

If you're a mom just like me who has been through this shit and wants to help others, you can also sign up for a training and learn how to do that. It's not free, but few things in this world are.

Another thing you can do - that typically is free or at least affordable - is Mental Health First Aid, which I hope becomes as prevalent as CPR and other first aid courses. This class teaches you how to identify someone in emotional distress and how to help them, who to call for help, and more. It's an amazing resource for people in the healthcare profession, anyone who works in any service industry, or those who work in an office where you're around people. Heck, it's just good for everyone to have. You could be in the grocery store one day, and someone could have a panic attack in the middle of an aisle. It'd be nice to know how to help them.

No one is immune from mental health disorders, and they can strike at any time. It's nice to know how to help people, so they actually get the help they need and aren't just taken off in a cop car to wait in jail until they calm down. Mental health is so misunderstood, and it's classes like this that are educating people and giving law enforcement, healthcare professionals, and people in general a glimpse into the complexity of the human mind and the spectrum of mental health disorders.

To find a class near you or to sign up to become an instructor, visit https://www.mentalhealthfirstaid.org/. If your office, hospital, or company hasn't offered employees an opportunity to take a Mental Health First Aid class yet, you can talk to your HR person to get something coordinated!

We can all do more when we're armed with the information to do so.

Chapter 13:

You've got this

This chapter is for anyone affected by these disorders: moms, dads, and kids, you've got this. I know it doesn't feel like it. I know it sucks when people tell you, "Have hope," "This is just a phase," or, "Think positively." I've wanted to punch people for saying all three.

This all feels hopeless, hard, and dark. That's OK. I want you all to trust that you've got this. It's not going to be easy. It's not going to be pretty. And it's not going to be quick. I've met some moms who feel "normal" nine months into motherhood. I know moms that just had the baby blues and were able to enjoy the rest of the newborn phase. I also know moms that are still dealing with their illness years later - myself included. What's important is that they're still working on it. This is a marathon, not a sprint, and I'm sorry for that.

You are not alone. Let me say that again: you are not alone! There are women all over the world - especially here in the

U.S. - who are struggling with this. You are normal, and what you're feeling with these disorders is normal. Those scary thoughts: normal. The rage: normal. This struggle: normal. And you will come out of this onto the other side.

Please don't beat yourself up for having a shit day, week, or month. No one cares that it's been a few days since you've showered or that the dishes are piling up in the sink. Did you wake up and take care of the kids today, make sure you ate something, and maybe brush your teeth? That's enough. Did you simply just wake up today and make sure the kids were fed? That's enough. Did you go to work, pump, and come home exhausted at the end of the day? You're a fucking boss. You're a fucking boss for showing up every single day - at work or at home. And if you just suffered a miscarriage but got up out of bed and still did anything you needed to do, you're incredible. You are a woman. Your body and your mind were made for incredible things. While your brain may be slow to catch up to this greatness, it will catch back up. With therapy, medication, and whatever else works for you, your brain will get back. Soon your body and your brain will start going through the motions together instead of seemingly fighting each other on a daily basis.

You'll have setbacks. You'll have bumps and moments of rage

you didn't see coming, but you'll be more like yourself again, and that's what's important. Bad days are just part of the process, so don't beat yourself up.

And for anyone who needs to hear this: **You are loved. You are wanted. You are worthy. You are strong. You are a fucking goddess. You've got this.**

Chapter 14:

Refrences

Chapter 1:

Watkins, S., et al. Early breastfeeding experiences and postpartum depression. (Aug. 2011). Obstetrics and Gynecology, 2(1), 214-221. doi: 10.1097/ AOG.0b013e3182260a2d.

Johns Hopkins Medicine. Hormone Levels May Predict Postpartum Depression. (Jun. 19, 2018). Retrieved from www.hopkinsmedicine.org/news/articles/hormone-levels-may-predict-postpartum-depression.

Chapter 2:

National Institute of Mental Health. Postpartum Depression Facts. Retrieved Dec. 2019, from https://www.nimh.nih.gov/health/publications/postpartum-depression-facts/index.shtml.

Chapter 3 (references for screening guidelines):

U.S. Preventive Services Task Force. Final Recommendation Statement: Depression in Adults: Screening. (May 2019). Retrieved from www.uspreventiveservicestaskforce.org/Page/Document/RecommendationStatementFinal/depression-in-adults-screening1.

Davidson, JR. Meltzer-Brody, SE. The underrecognition and undertreatment of depression: what is the breadth and depth of the problem? (1999). Journal of Clinical Psychiatry, 60(7), 4-9. Retrieved from www.ncbi.nlm.nih.gov/pubmed/10326869.

Earls, MF. Incorporating Recognition and Management of Perinatal and Postpartum Depression Into Pediatric Practice. (Nov. 2010). Pediatrics, 126(5),1032-1039. https://doi.org/10.1542/peds.2010-2348.

Flynn, HA., Blow, FC., Marcus, SM. Rates and predictors of depression treatment among pregnant women in hospital-affiliated obstetrics practices. (July 2006). General Hospital Psychiatry, 28(4), 289-295. 10.1016/j.genhosppsych.2006.04.002.

Gavin, NI., et al. Perinatal depression: A systematic review of prevalence and incidence. (Nov. 2005). Obstetrics & Gynecology, 106(5, Pt. 1), 1071-1083. doi: 10.1097/01.AOG.0000183597.31630.db.

Matthey, S., et al. Validation of the Edinburgh Postnatal Depression Scale for men, and comparison of item endorsement with their partners. (May 2001). Journal of Affective Disorders, 64(2-3), 175-184. doi: 10.1016/s0165-0327(00)00236-6.

American College of Obstetricians and Gynecologists. Screening for Perinatal Depression. (October 24, 2018). Retrieved from www.acog.org/Clinical-Guidance-and-Publications/Committee-Opinions/Committee-on-Obstetric-Practice/Screening-for-Perinatal-Depression.

Weissman, MM., et al. Remission in maternal depression and child psychopathology. A Star*D-child report. (Mar. 2006). JAMA, 295(12),1389-1398. doi: 10.1001/jama.295.12.1389.

Wisner, KL., O'Hara, MW. Perinatal mental illness:
definition, description and aetiology. (Jan. 2014). Best
Practice & Research Clinical Obstetetrics & Gynaecology,
18(1), 3-12. doi: 10.1016/j.bpobgyn.2013.09.002.

Chapter 4:

Fitelson, E., et al. Treatment of postpartum depression:
clinical, psychological and pharmacological options.
(2011). International Journal of Women's Health, 3, 1-14.
doi: 10.2147/IJWH.S6938.

Rysavy, MB. Sadness and Support: A Short History of
Postpartum Depression. (May 3, 2013). University of Iowa
Robert Sparks Essay Contest. Retrieved from https://
medicine.uiowa.edu/bioethics/bioethics/sites/medicine.
uiowa.edu.bioethics/files/wysiwyg_uploads/2013%20
Rysavy%20essay.pdf.

Chapter 11:

Flanders-Stpans, MB. Alarming Racial Differences
in Maternal Mortality. (2000). Journal of Perinatal
Education, 9(2), 50-51. doi: 10.1624/105812400X87653.

Neighmond, P. Why Racial Gaps In Maternal Mortality Persist. (May 10, 2019). National Public Radio. Retrieved from https://www.npr.org/sections/health-shots/2019/05/10/722143121/why-racial-gaps-in-maternal-mortality-persist.

The Economist. What disasters reveal about mental-health care. (Mar. 16, 2019). Retrieved from https://www.economist.com/international/2019/03/16/what-disasters-reveal-about-mental-health-care.

Lindahl, Pearson and Colpe. Prevalence of Suicidality During Pregnancy and the Postpartum (May 11, 2005) National institutes of Mental Health, Bethesda, MD. https://link.springer.com/article/10.1007%2Fs00737-005-0080-1

Goldman-Mellor, Margerison. Maternal drug-related death and suicide are leading causes of postpartum death in California (Novemner 2019, Volume 221, Issue 5, Pages 489.e1–489.e9) American Journal of Obstetrics and Gynecology

Edinburgh Postnatal Depression Scale[1] (EPDS)

Name: ________________________________   Address: ______________________________

Your Date of Birth: _____________________   ______________________________

Baby's Date of Birth: ___________________   Phone: ______________________________

As you are pregnant or have recently had a baby, we would like to know how you are feeling. Please check the answer that comes closest to how you have felt **IN THE PAST 7 DAYS**, not just how you feel today.

Here is an example, already completed.

I have felt happy:
- ☐ Yes, all the time
- ☒ Yes, most of the time   This would mean: "I have felt happy most of the time" during the past week.
- ☐ No, not very often   Please complete the other questions in the same way.
- ☐ No, not at all

In the past 7 days:

1. I have been able to laugh and see the funny side of things
- ☐ As much as I always could
- ☐ Not quite so much now
- ☐ Definitely not so much now
- ☐ Not at all

2. I have looked forward with enjoyment to things
- ☐ As much as I ever did
- ☐ Rather less than I used to
- ☐ Definitely less than I used to
- ☐ Hardly at all

*3. I have blamed myself unnecessarily when things went wrong
- ☐ Yes, most of the time
- ☐ Yes, some of the time
- ☐ Not very often
- ☐ No, never

4. I have been anxious or worried for no good reason
- ☐ No, not at all
- ☐ Hardly ever
- ☐ Yes, sometimes
- ☐ Yes, very often

*5 I have felt scared or panicky for no very good reason
- ☐ Yes, quite a lot
- ☐ Yes, sometimes
- ☐ No, not much
- ☐ No, not at all

*6. Things have been getting on top of me
- ☐ Yes, most of the time I haven't been able to cope at all
- ☐ Yes, sometimes I haven't been coping as well as usual
- ☐ No, most of the time I have coped quite well
- ☐ No, I have been coping as well as ever

*7 I have been so unhappy that I have had difficulty sleeping
- ☐ Yes, most of the time
- ☐ Yes, sometimes
- ☐ Not very often
- ☐ No, not at all

*8 I have felt sad or miserable
- ☐ Yes, most of the time
- ☐ Yes, quite often
- ☐ Not very often
- ☐ No, not at all

*9 I have been so unhappy that I have been crying
- ☐ Yes, most of the time
- ☐ Yes, quite often
- ☐ Only occasionally
- ☐ No, never

*10 The thought of harming myself has occurred to me
- ☐ Yes, quite often
- ☐ Sometimes
- ☐ Hardly ever
- ☐ Never

Administered/Reviewed by _______________________________ Date _______________________________

[1] Source: Cox, J.L., Holden, J.M., and Sagovsky, R. 1987. Detection of postnatal depression: Development of the 10-item Edinburgh Postnatal Depression Scale.   *British Journal of Psychiatry* 150:782-786 .

[2] Source: K. L. Wisner, B. L. Parry, C. M. Piontek, Postpartum Depression N Engl J Med vol. 347, No 3, July 18, 2002, 194-199

Edinburgh Postnatal Depression Scale[1] (EPDS)

Postpartum depression is the most common complication of childbearing.[2] The 10-question Edinburgh Postnatal Depression Scale (EPDS) is a valuable and efficient way of identifying patients at risk for "perinatal" depression. The EPDS is easy to administer and has proven to be an effective screening tool.

Mothers who score above 13 are likely to be suffering from a depressive illness of varying severity. The EPDS score should not override clinical judgment. A careful clinical assessment should be carried out to confirm the diagnosis. The scale indicates how the mother has felt *during the previous week*. In doubtful cases it may be useful to repeat the tool after 2 weeks. The scale will not detect mothers with anxiety neuroses, phobias or personality disorders.

Women with postpartum depression need not feel alone. They may find useful information on the web sites of the National Women's Health Information Center <www.4women.gov> and from groups such as Postpartum Support International <www.chss.iup.edu/postpartum> and Depression after Delivery <www.depressionafterdelivery.com>.

SCORING

QUESTIONS 1, 2, & 4 (without an *)
Are scored 0, 1, 2 or 3 with top box scored as 0 and the bottom box scored as 3.

QUESTIONS 3, 5-10 (marked with an *)
Are reverse scored, with the top box scored as a 3 and the bottom box scored as 0.

Maximum score: 30
Possible Depression: 10 or greater
Always look at item 10 (suicidal thoughts)

Users may reproduce the scale without further permission, providing they respect copyright by quoting the names of the authors, the title, and the source of the paper in all reproduced copies.

Instructions for using the Edinburgh Postnatal Depression Scale:

1. The mother is asked to check the response that comes closest to how she has been feeling in the previous 7 days.

2. All the items must be completed.

3. Care should be taken to avoid the possibility of the mother discussing her answers with others. (Answers come from the mother or pregnant woman.)

4. The mother should complete the scale herself, unless she has limited English or has difficulty with reading.

[1]Source: Cox, J.L., Holden, J.M., and Sagovsky, R. 1987. Detection of postnatal depression: Development of the 10-item Edinburgh Postnatal Depression Scale. *British Journal of Psychiatry* 150:782-786.

[2]Source: K. L. Wisner, B. L. Parry, C. M. Piontek, Postpartum Depression N Engl J Med vol. 347, No 3, July 18, 2002, 194-199

PATIENT HEALTH QUESTIONNAIRE (PHQ-9)

NAME:____ DATE:______________

Over the last *2 weeks,* how often have you been bothered by any of the following problems?
(use "✓" to indicate your answer)

	Not at all	Several days	More than half the days	Nearly every day
1. Little interest or pleasure in doing things	0	1	2	3
2. Feeling down, depressed, or hopeless	0	1	2	3
3. Trouble falling or staying asleep, or sleeping too much	0	1	2	3
4. Feeling tired or having little energy	0	1	2	3
5. Poor appetite or overeating	0	1	2	3
6. Feeling bad about yourself—or that you are a failure or have let yourself or your family down	0	1	2	3
7. Trouble concentrating on things, such as reading the newspaper or watching television	0	1	2	3
8. Moving or speaking so slowly that other people could have noticed. Or the opposite — being so figety or restless that you have been moving around a lot more than usual	0	1	2	3
9. Thoughts that you would be better off dead, or of hurting yourself	0	1	2	3

add columns   +   +

(Healthcare professional: For interpretation of TOTAL,   TOTAL: _________
please refer to accompanying scoring card).

10. If you checked off *any problems,* how *difficult* have these problems made it for you to do your work, take care of things at home, or get along with other people?	Not difficult at all	_________
	Somewhat difficult	_________
	Very difficult	_________
	Extremely difficult	_________

PHQ-9 Patient Depression Questionnaire

For initial diagnosis:

1. Patient completes PHQ-9 Quick Depression Assessment.
2. If there are at least 4 ✓s in the shaded section (including Questions #1 and #2), consider a depressive disorder. Add score to determine severity.

Consider Major Depressive Disorder

- if there are at least 5 ✓s in the shaded section (one of which corresponds to Question #1 or #2)

Consider Other Depressive Disorder

- if there are 2-4 ✓s in the shaded section (one of which corresponds to Question #1 or #2)

Note: Since the questionnaire relies on patient self-report, all responses should be verified by the clinician, and a definitive diagnosis is made on clinical grounds taking into account how well the patient understood the questionnaire, as well as other relevant information from the patient.
Diagnoses of Major Depressive Disorder or Other Depressive Disorder also require impairment of social, occupational, or other important areas of functioning (Question #10) and ruling out normal bereavement, a history of a Manic Episode (Bipolar Disorder), and a physical disorder, medication, or other drug as the biological cause of the depressive symptoms.

To monitor severity over time for newly diagnosed patients or patients in current treatment for depression:

1. Patients may complete questionnaires at baseline and at regular intervals (eg, every 2 weeks) at home and bring them in at their next appointment for scoring or they may complete the questionnaire during each scheduled appointment.
2. Add up ✓s by column. For every ✓: Several days = 1 More than half the days = 2 Nearly every day = 3
3. Add together column scores to get a TOTAL score.
4. Refer to the accompanying **PHQ-9 Scoring Box** to interpret the TOTAL score.
5. Results may be included in patient files to assist you in setting up a treatment goal, determining degree of response, as well as guiding treatment intervention.

Scoring: add up all checked boxes on PHQ-9

For every ✓ Not at all = 0; Several days = 1;
More than half the days = 2; Nearly every day = 3

Interpretation of Total Score

Total Score	Depression Severity
1-4	Minimal depression
5-9	Mild depression
10-14	Moderate depression
15-19	Moderately severe depression
20-27	Severe depression

A2662B 10-04-2005

Acknowledgments

This book would not have been written were it not for Mary Jo Simpson - my mother-in-law - who insisted that this book needed to exist and that I should be the one to make it happen. Thank you, also, to the women who so bravely shared their struggles for the benefit of others, to Abby Burd for sharing her professional insight, to John Simpson for designing my amazing cover, to Matt Clements for being my editor, and to my husband, Michael Simpson and my darling children Dean and Aefa, who have weathered this storm with me, every step of the way.

I also have to thank my therapists who have saved my life and helped me learn to enjoy being a mom: Dr. Thorne and Dr. Holzhauer in Charlotte, N.C., Dr. Thein in Lewsville, Texas, and Dr. Hart in Highland Village, Texas. Without these four women really listening and hearing what I was going through, and finding ways that worked for me to begin to heal, I'd be lost, or worse. So thank you.